LAME OF THRONES

Also by The Harvard Lampoon

Bored of the Rings

Nightlight

The Hunger Pains

The Wobbit

The Stoner's Guide to Landmark Tennessee Supreme
Court Cases pre-1860

Stay Inside the Lines, Behind Enemy Lines:
A Gulf War Coloring Book

Okay Expectations

Ass Wednesday

Where the Wild Thangs At?

Call of Duty: Black Ops

The United States Constitution Strategy Guide
(with Cheat Codes)

All of James Patterson's Books: The Book

Hamlette

Untitled surfing dog project

Barron Trump: A Star Wars *Story*

Curious George Sacrifices Ten to Save Thousands

The Anarchist's Eat, Pray, Love

Remember coins? Yeah, we invented those. Not a book.

To Revive a Mostly Deceased Mockingbird

Bram Stoker's Count Chocula

Doctor Boobs: Boobs Doctor

Danimal Farm

LAME OF THRONES

THE FINAL BOOK
IN A SONG OF
HOT AND COLD

— A PARODY —

THE HARVARD LAMPOON

NEW YORK

Hachette Books
Hachette Book Group
1290 Avenue of the Americas
New York, NY 10104
HachetteBooks.com
Twitter.com/HachetteBooks
Instagram.com/HachetteBooks

First Edition: November 2020

Published by Hachette Books, an imprint of Perseus Books, LLC, a subsidiary of Hachette Book Group, Inc. The Hachette Books name and logo is a trademark of the Hachette Book Group.

The Hachette Speakers Bureau provides a wide range of authors for speaking events.

To find out more, go to www.hachettespeakersbureau.com or call (866) 376-6591.

The publisher is not responsible for websites (or their content) that are not owned by the publisher.

Print book interior design by Six Red Marbles, Inc.

Interior art credit: Isabel Gibney and Nicole Araya

Library of Congress Cataloging-in-Publication Data has been applied for.

ISBNs: 978-0-306-87367-6 (trade paperback), 978-0-306-87370-6 (ebook)

Library of Congress Control Number: 2020935644

Printed in the United States of America

LSC-C

1 2020

For all the kids who dream about becoming authors themselves. Fat chance. Now that we're back in the book-writing game, nobody needs you.

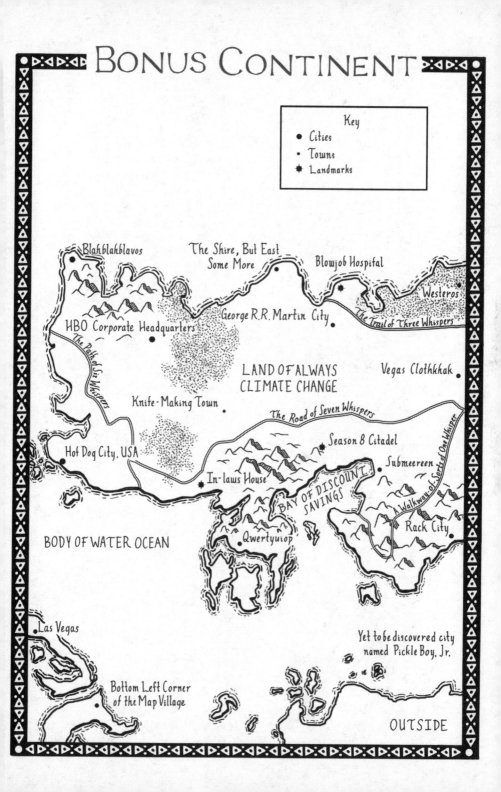

Preface from the Author

Dear Fans,

As I dictate this to you, I'm lounging in Cabo with
my feet on the biggest pair of knockers they've ever seen.
You gotta trust me on this, but these knockers make
the knockers on the TV version of Game of Thrones
look like the knockers in the book version of Game of
Thrones.

It's me: George R. R. Martin (net worth: $100 mil-
lion). If you're reading this, you probably don't have a
TV. I have nine TVs—and that's not even counting
my tenth TV. I'm, how do I put this delicately, really

goshdarn fucking rich now. Why is this? Well, let me tell you.

It's summer 1996, and I'm on the Strip. I open up my typewriter, make sure my ink ribbon is full, and realize my rampant, unrelatable obsession with fantasy is a nonissue. I should write a book about dragons, *I think. I black in two months later, and somehow my fifteen-page pop-up children's book about dragons has become a nine-hundred-page pop-up children's book about dragons.* Shit shit shit! Too long, George! Too long!

Yada yada yada, my editor got rid of the pop-ups, made me add more human sex, cut two hundred consecutive pages that were just last names of all the barbers in the Game of Thrones *universe, and that's basically the first novel you've all come to know and love!*

Fast-forward 25 years. Fast-forward 100 more years. Now rewind 102 years. It's 2019, and HBO has turned my book series into the preeminent softcore porn series. At this point, I'm rich as a mother-effing motherfucker. I haven't seen the show in years, but my friends describe the episodes to me. Sounds pretty good. Sounds exactly like how I would've done it. But now they want me to finish off these damn books.

Now look, I really wish I could end this series with a forty-five-slide PowerPoint, but fans always complain to me when I don't wrap up each character's story arc in a fulfilling way. Apparently, I introduced a character called "Trashbag" in the second book and never mentioned him again. I am accosted about the fate of this character on a weekly basis. Did you know I have introduced over three thousand characters in the novels who collectively have four thousand individual boobs with their own storylines? And as if I didn't have that many boobs on my plate, imagine what would happen if I didn't wrap up the character arc of the main guy in the books! The guy I killed. What's his name? Tom? Tom Something? Tom?

I have been told repeatedly that it's taken me over a decade to write this book, and it's likely that many of my fans have forgotten some of the plot points during that time. Personally, I have never read a preface or a prologue or an introduction or an author's note in my life. I just skip to the book and deal with the ensuing confusion like an adult. For the sake of the children who read my dragon erotica, however, I will try to recap the plot as best I can. Jon! Dammit! That's his name, not Tom. Oh God, did I write the whole book calling him Tom? Okay, if I did that, every time you see "Tom" just replace it with "Jon."

So yeah, Jon Dough is the main guy, yeah? What's up with him? Ah, right. I've got to stop killing the main characters every time I get the itch. Speaking of which, Chauncibell, when you get a moment, fetch some more of my talcum powder. *Okay, so Jon was the Bored Demander of the Night's Crotch, which means he was basically in charge of the guys who defend the Trench. Of course the Trench is some sort of magical thing up north, built to keep out the Mildlings. Trench? No, was it a trench, it was… Yes. Yes, it was a Trench, must've been. The White Wieners and the zombos, they're there too.* Chauncibell, this is real talcum powder. Yes, I know I said "itch." But do I look itchy to you? I am a model of cleanliness and health. When I said talcum powder I meant another mimosa. You should be able to anticipate my needs regardless of what I ask for. *White Wieners and the zombos and they're led by… the White Wieners and the zombos are led by…* Come on, George, come on, man.

The Nighty Night King! Right. And Jon saved all these Mildlings from him and brought them south of the Trench to Casablacka with the Night's Crotch. Some of the guys in the Night's Crotch got really mad about that and all stabbed Jon. Now he's dead. Unless… it was all a dream! A dream? And there never was a Game of Thrones, *and the little kid dreaming the dream went back to sleep and lived happily ever after?*

Wait, no, George, you've tried this before, and every time your editor says, "The dream ending will not appease fans. It's a cop out. You will become poor again." So here we go, what else, what else?

There's this witch named Smellisandre. There's also Jon's huge best friend Whoremund, who is a Mildling. Not his other huge best friend, the fat book guy. Ham? Hamuel? Hamwell Tardy? Eddddd, my man, from the Night's Crotch is there, and he thinks he's Jon's best friend too. Just let him believe that. And finally, there's this smuggler named Ser Boats McSeaman who was trying to learn how to read and used to be second in command for Stankass Boaratheon. Basically those four people and also Jon's direwolf, Toast, are all just sort of locked in this room at Casablacka with Jon's dead body? What are they going to do about it? He's dead, okay? Unless, no. Fuck. Did I already try the dream thing?

Whatever, he's dead right now. One storyline down. I really just want to apologize about how many characters there are, folks. That was, you know, I really went overboard with the characters. It's too many. Okay? You all know Dennys Grandslam. She's also the main character. Very pretty. Silver hair. I want to touch the hair. All she cares about is eventually sitting on the Pointy Chair and becoming queen of Westopolis, and so to help her do that, she freed the city of Submeereen, which is not actually in Westopolis, and she tried to install a government there by crucifying the former slavemasters and listening to individual complaints one after another in a pyramid. I don't know, guys, I was high for most of the nineties. Anyway, she freed the slaves, and the old slave owners were mad. So mad, they besieged the city, and then Dennys got kidnapped by the Clothkhaki. Funny story, I came up with the entire Clothkhaki language by sneaking drugs into my butler Chauncibell's food and recording the sounds he made.

Now Peter Dinklage is running Submeereen with Ms. Andei (the translator) and Dog Shit (the

Funsullied leader). Shit, Beerion. Not Peter Dinklage, that's the . . . eh—whatever, copyediting will catch that before this gets published. Dennys's dragons are locked up in a basement.

Let's go, I don't know, north now. Bland Snark. Bland is the handicapped kid. What else is there to say? He has visions and is hiding in a huge old tree north of the Trench with a wise man called the Pink-Eyed Raven, who is teaching him to be better at having visions. Bland overcompensates for his broken legs by doing a lot of upper-body exercises. Is that true? I cannot remember if that's explained in the first four thousand pages of the Game of Thrones *series, but I remember wanting that to be true. If it's not there, I'm just deciding now that it's still canon. I declare it . . . true!*

Then there's the main character, Cervix Bangsister. She was the queen of Westopolis until her husband died, so her son Jeffy became king, and then he died, and now her son Timid is king. She hates Timid's wife, Manmeat Thighspell, because she gets to be queen instead of Cervix and also because she gets to have sex with Timid instead of her. Cervix is in King's Landing Strip now and just got in trouble with the religious freaks there. The Beaky Buzzards, I calls 'em. Scariest cult any writer has ever written! I once got in trouble with a church, oh yes. A priest caught me impersonating him in the confessional booth. I heard forty confessions, and I wrotes 'em all down! Forty confessions is forty more intimate personal stories that I can turn into eight hundred more characters for me to use in me books!

Anywho, Cervix won't confess for doing incest with her brother, Ser Lemme Bangsister. God, the forty-five-slide PowerPoint ending sounds so tempting right about now. Why, George? Why all the characters? You just couldn't stop could you. Introduced that dumbass character "Trashbag" just because you were bored and out of coke. You're paying for it now, George, huh?

Lemme got kidnapped and got his butt cut off. No, not his butt. Hahaha, could you imagine? How could I possibly have a character without a butt? That wouldn't be hot at all. Hahaha, imagine that. A character without a butt? Preposterous! Lemme actually got his head cut off, and even though it's been replaced by a prosthetic gold head, it's put a strain on most facets of his life. Lemme also hangs out with my man LeBronn, the sellsword. If there is one character I can see myself in, it's gotta be him. He, similarly to me, is just so sick. He's so cool. He's—he's just the man. He's the best character by far and secretly the main character. You'll see.

Okay, think, think, think. Characters, Georgie, characters. *Uhhhh…Gorlon? No, that's not one. Hmmmm…Malarya? Malarya Snark. Yeah, that's one of them. Okay, she's gross and loves violence. She's way out in Blahblahblahvos training to be even better at violence. Her sister Pantsa is the spoiled, hot one of questionable age. Littledingle convinced Pantsa to marry Handsy Boytoy, that misunderstood guy with the dogs. Last we heard from her, I had her jump off a castle and not die by landing in a few inches of snow. Now she's free, baby!!! Pantsa Snark is on the loose, everybody!*

Who else? Someone name a character. Anyone. God these mimosas are bottomless as hell. Yes, one more please. Chauncibell! I'm on a roll here, man, bring me my catheter so I don't have to get up to go to the bathroom. I'm definitely forgetting at least half of the storylines. I feel like there's a wizard or something? A teenage wizard with a unique scar, maybe? Or, like, a cat with a big personality? Ahhhhhh, screw it. You guys will figure it out.

Anyway, I present you with the final book. *I hope you enjoy reading it as much as I am enjoying this handjob right now that I paid for with your money.*

Best,

Georgie

LAME OF THRONES

Jon

This book sucks!" screamed Ser Boats McSeaman, hurling said book across the room. It could have been full of spells for bringing people back to life, but the lack of pictures and fun reading-comprehension questions made it unintelligible to Boats. Once again his inability to read had prevented him from reading. He was furious.

Boats huddled over Jon Dough's corpse. Knocks continued to pound on the heavy oak door that stood as the only defense between Jon's allies and the traitors who had taken over Casablacka and killed their own Bored Demander of the Night's Crotch.

"Everything is pointless, and we're all gonna die," said Eddddd in his low monotone. Boats punched him clear across the room and into a corner, still angered by all the time he'd wasted trying to read the spell book.

"Perhaps I can try one of my spells. I have seen dead men brought back to life before, and though my morale is low since I haven't set anyone on fire in so long, there is a chance I can still help Jon" is what Smellisandre would have said if Boats hadn't hurled three bookcases at her in the middle of the first word. Boats rampaged around the room, destroying every written word in sight. He even ripped a beam out of the ceiling because it sort of resembled the letter *I*.

Whoremund, who had been sleeping off the fermented hog urine he drank not ten minutes before, was awakened by the sound of Boats ripping ten books in half at once with his teeth. Whoremund immediately joined in, savaging every book he could find without asking any questions. While Ser Boats and Whoremund ripped up every instance of the written word they could find, Smellisandre scrambled to her feet and raced to revive Jon before Boats noticed that she looked like a lowercase *t* if she held her arms out to the side. She took a deep breath and began:

> *"O Fire Man,*
> *Father of all,*
> *Put down that beer*
> *And hear my call.*
> *You see this kid here?*
> *'Jon,' I think?*
> *Please make him not dead.*

He's starting to stink.
So stick out your hip
And swing your hair.
Shake that rump like you just don't care.
Hand me the codeine, hand me the Sprite.
Let's go, Seahawks. Fight, fight, fight."

Toast, Jon's faithful direwolf, looked hopefully at his master. But nothing happened. Smellisandre turned away and looked sadly at Whoremund and Boats. They looked at Jon, then at Smellisandre, then back at Jon, then at each other; then Whoremund looked at Jon while Boats kept staring at Whoremund. Then Smellisandre stared at the person to the left of her, who was on Whoremund's right and was perpendicular to Toast. Who was the person?

It was hopeless. Whoremund, Boats, and Smellisandre started to leave the room when they heard a shuffling from behind them. They turned to Jon's body and saw his chest rising and falling. This turned out to be a rat gnawing at Jon's cold, dead ribcage underneath his shirt. Disappointed, they started opening the door when they heard a "Gosh, wow, I'm alive again! I really am!" But it was just the wind.

As the three of them continued for the door, Jon suddenly whipped back into life with one quick breath, but Whoremund was the only one who noticed. Whoremund jumped and shrieked like a little girl. Everyone started laughing at Whoremund since it looked like he was freaking out for no reason. Eddddd laughed so hard, he peed his pants and then draped them over Whoremund's face and called him a little pee boy. Smellisandre laughed so hard she gave Whoremund a wedgie and then burned a kid alive who was standing outside.

"Gosh, wow, I'm alive again! I really am!" the wind whistled again. Jon shut the window so the breeze wouldn't drown him out. "You guys, I can't believe it! You brought me back"—Jon went in for one of his trademark group hugs but slipped on the blood from his wounds, slid across the room, and impaled himself on a sword—"to life!" he managed to croak before passing away.

⁓⁑⁓

"Hahaha, miss me already?" said Jon to Whoremund and Boats as they tried desperately to keep the door shut and hold off the traitors. Smellisandre got up from where she was reciting her spells, hoping nobody noticed that she got so scared when Jon woke up again for the second time that she herself had peed in her pants a little bit.

"Jon, you need to be more careful. I may not be able to bring you back again. I don't know how much power I have here in the North, and without people to burn . . . people to burn . . . people . . . burn . . . Mildlings . . . burn Mildlings . . ." Smellisandre panted, her pupils dilating, a wild smile forming on her face.

"The Mildlings! Of course, how could I forget!" yelled Jon. "They must be so worried without me!" Jon pulled Whoremund with him toward the door. "Whoremund, we must go see your people! They need to know that I've been brought back"—Jon kicked open the door and came face-to-face with his assassins, Asserhole Thorn, Fucknugget, and Orphan Kid, who had been waiting outside the room this whole time. Asserhole immediately stabbed him in the heart—"to life!" Jon managed to croak before passing away.

⸎

"You know what they say, fourth life's the charm!" laughed Jon as Whoremund cradled Boats, who was rapidly losing blood. The assassins were tied up on the ground, bleeding heavily from the fight that had ensued after Jon died again. A crowd of Mildlings and Brothers of the Night's Crotch had gathered. They gawked at the newly revived Jon.

"What do you want us to do with these traitors?" asked Smellisandre.

"Ahhh, just let 'em go so we can toss the ol' pigskin around like we used to" is what Jon wanted to say. Surely that is what his father would have done. But Jon was conflicted. He knew his men wanted justice for the traitors who had killed their leader. *On the one hand, they did kill me, the Bored Demander of the Night's Crotch, twice*, he thought. *But on the other hand, it suuuuuure has been a*

5

while since we tossed the pigskin. Jon looked to Toast for guidance, but he knew that would be of no use. Toast loved the pigskin more than anyone.

Jon decided that his best shot at an answer would be to ask the Seven Gods. Perhaps they could share some hidden wisdom. *O Gods, hear my plea*, thought Jon. *I request an audience with you all: The Father, the Mother, the Hamburglar, Officer Big Mac, Mayor McCheese, Grimace, the Chicken McNuggmonster, Dr. McFlurry, Auntie Cheese, and any of the other Seven Gods I forgot to mention. My Brothers ask what is to be done with these three prisoners before me—prisoners we have long called Brothers, who have fought fiercely beside us to guard the Trench. What am I to do?*

For a moment all was still. Then Jon's head erupted with the sounds of the Seven arguing among themselves like usual. *The burgers are all mine! No, they're mine! Hey, who turned out the lights? I'm a dad, I'm a dad, I'm the father! Oooookkaayy, who ordered the Nuggmonster? Jesus, I deserve better than this. I'm a doctor for Christ's sake! Wait, who's Christ? I'm Auntie Cheese!* Jon didn't know what to make of this. But then one voice rose above the rest, calming and pure. Jon knew that voice. It had brought him comfort in his darkest moments and showed him the path when he was most lost. It was the low baritone of Officer Big Mac, shepherd of justice, lord of law enforcement.

Jon, spurted Officer Big Mac from somewhere between his two all-beef patties slathered with special sauce. *Your* men deserve the justice they elected you to provide. These three traitors are not worthy of the black they wear. They are not worthy of the oaths they swore. They are not worthy of the air they continue to breathe. Officer Big Mac's words struck a chord in Jon, but he was not sure these were the words he wanted to hear. Officer Big Mac continued, You must make an example of these men. Take them to the gallows and lay their souls bare for all to see—oh my, what is that?

Just then Jon had conjured an image of the pigskin in his mind. Pretty swell, huh? thought Jon.

Fuck. Perhaps this is not as cut-and-dry as I thought, said Officer Big Mac, his lips salivating. No, no! We must stay focused on the task at hand, he said. Officer Big Mac sucked the saliva back into his mouth, regained his composure, and continued. Those traitors must be executed. And you must be the one who does it. The world will gain nothing through your mercy today. You are the 998th in an unbroken line of honorable men—men who rose to do what was right, despite any apprehensions. You are the 998th Bored Demander of the Night's Crotch. And you are the son of Deaddard Snark. He raised you to be loyal, to be true. If you let these traitors go, you will not only betray the Night's Crotch. You will betray your father's memory. And you will betray the people of Westopolis—the very people you've sworn to protect. Now go, Jon. Go and do what needs to be done.

Jon looked out at the sea of faces. Theirs were the faces of a people long starved of justice. A people possessed of a dwindling hope. He needed to show them that the world was not devoid of order. That so long as there was even a single man still sworn to uphold the laws of Gods and men, all would not be lost. He needed to be a leader.

Jon began, "I, Jon Dough, Bored Demander of the Night's Crotch, Defender of Westopolis, Watcher of the Trench, do sentence these men—"

"Oy, everybody! Look at the Bored Demander's crotch!" screamed someone in the crowd.

Jon looked down at his pants and saw an enormous wet spot.

"Oy, lads, he's had himself a wet dream while he was dead!"

Laughter filled the courtyard of Casablacka. The Brothers of the Night's Crotch were beside themselves. Jon looked to his friends, but they were all rolling on the ground, weak with laughter. Desperate, Jon looked to Toast for support—but the direwolf had donned a fake mustache so as not to be associated with the humiliated Bored Demander.

"Hey! Everyone listen to me! I'm going to execute the traitors!" shouted Jon. But his voice cracked in the middle of every word. The crowd absolutely lost it. Jon was more flustered than ever, the Seven Gods were struggling to contain their laughter, and even Toast couldn't help but look at Jon and raise his eyebrows as if to say, *Well, if this ain't just a bitch.*

Jon stormed over to Whoremund and Boats and hoisted them to their feet. "Help me bring these prisoners to the gallows!" Jon screamed. Whoremund and Boats somehow found the strength to suppress their laughter somewhat and lift up the assassins, who were squirming and laughing the hardest of all. Jon led Whoremund and Boats up the gallows steps, and he instructed them to place the assassins on the trap doors.

"People!" shouted Jon at the crowd. No one listened. "Hey! Everyone!" he tried again. Still nothing. Out of options, he did the only thing he could in this situation. He raised Casablacka's prized football in one hand and held a knife to it with the other.

Instantly the crowd quieted down. "That's better," said Jon. He put the pigskin away and began once more, "I, Jon Dough, Bored Demander of the Night's Crotch, Defender of Westopolis, Watcher of the Trench, hereto-forth notwithstanding hencewith, and subject to the terms and conditions, do sentence these three traitors to death." He paused for a moment. "But I will not hang them."

Murmurs could be heard from the crowd. "But you're the Bored Demander! You have to execute them!" screamed someone in the crowd, who then threw a big clump of dirt at Jon's head. The rest of the crowd joined in, throwing whatever they could get their hands on. Someone threw Eddddd, but he didn't fly nearly far enough and hit the ground really hard.

"Hey! Ow! Stop! I'm still going to kill them!" squealed Jon. He held up the football again. All the projectiles froze in midair and fell to the ground. The crowd was his once more.

"As I was *saying*, I will not hang them. Instead, I will allow them to choose the manner by which they will be made an example of today." The crowd was silent. "Meaning that I'm gonna kill them however they ask me to." The crowd went wild.

"First we'll start with Asserhole Thorn." Jon approached Asserhole, whose laughter from earlier finally seemed to be dying down. "Asserhole, you and I have never liked each other. You've always been super mean to me actually. To be honest, I've always secretly hoped that you could kill me twice so that I could kill you once in front of everybody. Now, how do you wish to die?"

Asserhole thought for a moment, and then smiled. "Sex," he said.

Jon was confused. "Uhhh, what do you mean?"

"I mean I want a horde of beautiful women to come and make incredible love to me until long after the point that I'm drained of semen, and then I'll die."

Jon looked disappointed. He'd really wanted to kill Asserhole for a long time. But a promise was a promise. "Very well, Asserhole. May the Gods have mercy on you."

Jon dispatched a few of his men to go to the nearest brothel and bring back forty women. When the women arrived, Jon explained Asserhole's wish to them, and they descended on him like piranhas swarming a cow. They had hot, sticky sex with him on the gallows for days. Jon recalled hearing that the human body could only go for three days without eating or drinking, so he'd been surprised to find Asserhole Thorn happily giving and receiving oral sex deep into day seven. On day eight the whores stepped away and revealed his dead body.

Next up was Fucknugget. "Fucknugget, you and I have never liked each other—"

"More sex," said Fucknugget.

Jon was dumbfounded. "Uhhhhhhh . . . what?"

"I want a shitload of hot broads to fuck me and make me cum buckets. I'm talking an absolute gaggle of women. Fifty times as many as Asserhole had. I want them to make me cum until I'm shooting blanks. And then I want to keep cumming until my body has no choice but to shoot my brain and my heart out of my penis, and then I want to cum some more. And once I'm done cumming I'll cum some more. And then I'll die."

Once again Jon had no choice but to keep his promise. He dispatched one hundred of his finest men to go back to the brothel and buy the whole place out. When they returned, Jon explained to the women what Fucknugget's wish was—this time using diagrams, mannequins, and some finger puppets when there weren't enough mannequins—and they got down to business. For eighty-three days they labored over Fucknugget's body as it slowly deteriorated. The crowd couldn't make out any of the details in the swirling mass of bodies; every once in a while a fleck of semen would fly out and arc across the courtyard of Casablacka, and every few days a random internal organ would fly out and hit someone in the eye. It was unclear at what point he died.

Finally it was time for Orphan Kid. This one would be the hardest of all. Jon had known Orphan Kid since way back when he was named Kid With A Family That Is Alive. It was Jon who supported the boy when he wanted to change his name to Orphan Kid because he thought it sounded cool. And when a year later his parents incidentally died, Jon was the only one who continued to call him Orphan Kid. Jon was like a father to him. But the boy had betrayed him.

"Orphan Kid, I want you to understand how hard this is for me," Jon said, stifling tears. "I always considered myself a father to you. Not *your* father. He's dead." Jon cast one last look at the boy. He was so small. So bright. He could have grown into a fine Brother. "But it's too late for that. Now, Orphan Kid...how do you wish to die?"

Orphan Kid somehow managed to hold back his tears, but a little poop still managed to slip out of him. He stood there thinking for what seemed like five hours, even though it was only a few, tops. Finally he looked up at Jon and spoke in his meek little voice. "Jon, I want to kill myself."

The crowd gasped. Whoremund, Boats, and Smellisandre looked sadly at the ground. Jon was honestly kinda bummed that he missed out on killing someone again.

"Jon, I know now that what I did was wrong. I shouldn't have killed you the first time. I probably shouldn't have killed you the second time either. And

I definitely shouldn't have laughed when it was obvious you had ejaculated in your pants and your voice cracked." The crowd started giggling at this last comment, but the boy continued. "I want to kill myself with the knife I used to stab you. I think it's only right that this is how I do penance for my crimes."

Jon was touched by Orphan Kid's decision. He had shown more grace and wisdom than his fellow conspirators, men ten times his age. "Very well, Orphan Kid. May the Gods have mercy on you." Jon untied Orphan Kid, but he didn't know where the knife was. Jon looked all around the gallows and the courtyard until he found the knife still sticking out of his chest. He pulled it out and handed it to Orphan Kid. "Haha, guess I forgot to remove it when I was brought back"—just then, Orphan Kid stabbed Jon in the heart again—"to life!" Jon managed to croak before collapsing dead.

❧

"Honey, I'm hooooome!" said Jon as the Brothers and Mildlings were stomping Orphan Kid into the ground. Jon batted them away and jerked Orphan Kid to his feet. "Alright Orphan Kid, veeeery funny. That was very funny what you did back there. That was actually really funny, I'm proud." Jon brushed the blood-encrusted hair off Orphan Kid's face and cast one last look at the boy—again. "But now, how do you really want to die?"

"The most sex," said Orphan Kid without missing a beat.

Jon would have face-palmed if only he weren't so confused again. "Uhhhhhhhhhhh—"

"I want three women for every man, woman, and child in the North, and I want them to make me shoot big gooey ropes of—"

"Okay, that's enough. You guys don't all have to describe it," said Jon. He got the gist of what Orphan Kid wanted. "Very well. May the Gods have mercy on you."

Jon dispatched every Brother and Mildling under his command to travel to all the brothels in the North and bring back every whore under the sun. When they returned to Casablacka, three hundred thousand whores in tow, Jon addressed them from the castle walls, where he had assembled a hundred local acting troupes—armed with all manner of costumes, props, paraphernalia, and lubricants—to demonstrate to the women how they were to go about killing this small boy. The show went on for several days, and after ten minutes of questions the women swarmed Casablacka and leapt onto Orphan Kid. He was dead within minutes. His flesh was stripped clean. The women took their payment and vanished into the horizon, never to be seen again.

Jon climbed down from the gallows and started walking back to his chambers when he heard a familiar voice from behind him. "Oh Jon, oh brother dear!" It was Jon's half sister, Pantsa Snark. He couldn't believe it. He hadn't seen or heard from her in years, not since the day he'd left their home castle of Wintersmells.

"Pantsa! By the Gods, you're alive!" Jon rushed to his sister and jumped to give her a hug—but she held him at arm's length and gestured for a firm handshake instead.

"Yes, yes, delightful to see you and all that," said Pantsa, who was frantically disinfecting the hand she had just used to touch her brother. She held one of her silk handkerchiefs to her nose and surveyed Casablacka, her face twisting into a grimace of disgust. "My, my! What a, um...fine castle this is, Jon." She looked her brother up and down and put a second handkerchief to her nose. "And you! You...you...you look, uh...well, I love how you just wear *anything*, Jon."

Jon smiled, happy at his sister's compliment. "Pantsa, what brings you up to the Trench? Don't you have to, uh..." Jon tried to remember the kinds of stuff his sister liked to do way back when they lived in Wintersmells. "Uhhh, don't you have to go find some leather to chew on? Those baby teeth should be coming in soon!" Jon was beaming, hoping his sister wouldn't call his bluff.

His sister looked puzzled. "Jon...my...baby teeth?" Jon smiled even harder but was starting to visibly sweat. "You...I...why, I just can't believe you remembered!" Pantsa opened her mouth to reveal her rows of white, well-maintained teeth and pointed to one little scraggly tooth poking through in the corner. "But that's not important right now. I came to the Trench because I need your help. Wintersmells has been taken by a cruel, cruel man named Handsy Boytoy. I was forced into marrying him and was kept as his captive, but I escaped. And now...I intend to return and take back our family castle."

Jon didn't know what to say. He still couldn't believe that baby teeth thing worked. "Pantsa, I can't leave the Night's Crotch. I was just killed and brought back to life—the Brothers can't bear to lose me again."

Pantsa looked behind Jon, where she saw the Brothers cooking, cleaning, helping one another, and developing advanced forms of technology and a flawless political system without Jon's help. "Jon, if what you say is true and you really did die, then your oath to the Night's Crotch is fulfilled. You're not a Brother anymore. And besides, the other Brothers are tough and independent. They can fare just fine without you."

Jon turned around and looked at the Brothers just as they were finishing up their first manned voyage to the moon. Maybe Pantsa was right. "But Pantsa, where are we going to find men to come and fight for Wintersmells? The Brothers need to stay and defend the Trench from the White Wieners and their army of zombos."

"The Mildlings, Jon. They are the toughest people in all of Westopolis, and they all look to you as a leader. If we don't get their help in the fight against Handsy, he and his men will come attack the Night's Crotch, and then there will be no one left to defend the realm from the White Wieners."

Jon looked over at the thousands of Mildlings who had gathered around a rat corpse and were taking turns licking it. *They sure are tough*, thought Jon. *But will that be enough...Haha, look at that, I made a rhyme without even trying.* Jon looked back at Pantsa and said, "Very well, sister. I'll come with you. There needs to be a Snark in Wintersmells. Just give me a moment."

Jon walked over to Eddddd, who was still lying motionless in the mud in front of the gallows. Jon shook his friend by the shoulders. "Eddddd! Edddddy, my friend! Wake up!"

Eddddd woke up, confused.

"Jon! I'm alive!" Eddddd shouted as Jon continued to shake him.

"Eddddd please stop making this about yourself. I have something very important to tell you. I'm leaving the Night's Crotch. I'm going to march south with the Mildling army to take back my family's castle. And I want you to be the new Bored Demander of the Night's Crotch."

Before Eddddd could protest, Jon peeled off all his clothes—the sacred uniform of the Bored Demander, still caked in blood from all the times he was killed—and threw them on top of Eddddd. Jon walked away as Eddddd suffocated under all the clothes that were blocking his airways.

Jon approached the Mildling camp, naked as his name day, and addressed the group. "Mildlings!" But they were too occupied by the rat corpse to listen. "Yoohoo, Mildlings!" Jon screamed as loud as he could, but there was no way they would hear him over the sounds of the particularly good licking the rat was getting right then. Jon ran up to the rat corpse and ate it in three large bites. The Mildlings were in awe.

"Mildlings! I am Jon Dough, the former Bored Demander of the Night's Crotch. I gave you safe passage over the Trench many moons ago and allowed you to live here at Casablacka, free of charge. Now I need your help. We all need to march south so that I can reclaim my family's castle. Most of you will probably die in horrific ways that you could never have even conceived of in the lands north of the Trench. Those who survive will most likely be subjected to the horrible racism and prejudice that the people of Westopolis feel toward your people. But that's okay, because I will have won back my castle. Now, who's with me?" Jon looked out at the Mildlings, but they stared back in shock. Jon wondered why they were so quiet—he thought he had given a pretty great speech—and then he realized that they were staring at the tail from the rat corpse, which was still stuck to his bottom lip. In one swift motion Jon slurped the rat tail into his mouth and swallowed all four feet of it whole, and the Mildlings erupted into cheers.

Jon approached the gates of Casablacka and looked to his friend Eddddd, who was still choking on Jon's clothes. "And now my crotch is splendid," said Jon. And just like that, he cast aside his brotherhood.

"Ammdnf mnow your crotfch isfff fffplendifff," said Eddddd from under the pile of bloody clothes.

18

Jon cast one last lingering look at Casablacka. He nodded at Toast, who had proudly taken off his fake moustache and replaced it with an "I'm Jon's dog" collar, and then he walked through the gates, naked, the Mildling army following close behind.

Bland

Bland Snark crouched behind a bush. It was a cool summer afternoon, and the steady murmur of a freshwater stream filled the air. At seven feet tall and 270 pounds of pure toned muscle, Bland's glorious, able-bodied figure was impossible to miss, but thanks to a powerful layer of magic, he was completely invisible to the beautiful young women running toward the water.

"Come on, girls! Last one in is a naughty, naughty pharaoh!"

"Wait for us, Cleopatra!"

The girls shed their tunics and splashed in the water, unaware of the thirteen-year-old boy heavily breathing from his mouth a few feet away. Bland watched them like a lion with a gazelle fetish watches a gazelle, until suddenly his concentration was broken by a piercing shriek.

The girls ran screaming into the forest as a hideously wrinkled little old man bubbled up to the surface and waddled out of the water, directly toward Bland. It was the Pink-Eyed Raven.

"Come, my child," he wheezed. "We don't have much time."

Bland's vision abruptly ended. He snapped back to reality and back into his pathetic crippled body, all crumpled up in his wheelchair. For the past month he had been living in the cave of the Pink-Eyed Raven, training in the magical art of *wanking*—the ability to view the past and the future and to inhabit the minds of others. Bland had shown promise in this art from a very young age, but the Pink-Eyed Raven claimed he could turn him into a master wank for just $60 per lesson.

"Let me go back! That was my best wank yet!" Bland yelled.

Encased in the large weirdwood tree at the center of the cave, the Pink-Eyed Raven rubbed his crusty eyes and wiped his hands on his slacks. "It's dangerous to stay in these visions for too long, Bland. What you saw back there—the beautiful women, the experience of having a body that is not gross and crippled like yours—these are not your destiny."

Bland wheeled himself away and furiously started doing pull-ups on one of the Pink-Eyed Raven's branches, without realizing that the old man seemed to get some sort of physical pleasure from this. Ever since his legs were paralyzed after a fall from a miniature horse at a carnival many years ago, Bland figured he could compensate for his disability by getting his upper body extraordinarily jacked. His direwolf, Scooby, whose legs were also paralyzed by a fall from a miniature horse's dog, wheeled himself up next to Bland in his dog wheelchair and spotted him. And off in the corner, busy trying to fit his fist inside his belly button, was the Snark family servant, Holdthedoorthezombosarecoming.

"Then what is my destiny?" Bland grunted between reps.

"Something much greater!" the Raven wheezed. "Someday you'll grow up to become just like me. And when I believe you're ready, I'll finally kill myself and you'll sit on top of my corpse in this tree for a billion years."

"I'm not doing that," said Bland.

"Holdthedoorthezombosarecoming," said Holdthedoorthezombosarecoming.

"But to prepare you, I must show you your past, present, and future," he said. And with that, the Pink-Eyed Raven placed his wrinkly hands on Bland's shoulders, and they transcended the fabric of time.

"Hey! What in the seven hells are you doing?" Bland said.

"I have to do this…It's part of the magic," said the Pink-Eyed Raven.

"Get your hands off me, man."

"Okay, okay, hold this tree branch then."

And with that, Bland placed his hand on the Pink-Eyed Raven's magic tree branch, and they transcended the fabric of time.

Bland would recognize the stench anywhere. They were in Wintersmells. The courtyard was bustling with people milling about, avoiding piles of manure scattered around the complex, slipping on piles of manure scattered around the complex. A cool, very handsome man was demonstrating how many backflips he could do to a group of off-the-clock prostitutes.

"Wow," said Bland. "So this is me in the future."

"No, no, that's Donny Slick. You haven't been born yet. The little punk crying in the pile of horseshit behind him is your father."

They watched young Deaddard Snark wipe the snot from his nose and pick himself up, then accidentally fall back into the pile of shit, then pick himself up again. He pulled his wooden toy sword out from an adjacent pile of shit, then accidentally fell back into the original pile of shit again. Finally a young girl came and helped him up. Bland recognized her as his aunt, Yomomma Snark.

"Don't cry, big brother," she said, helping him up from a different pile of shit he had just fallen into. "I'm sure those bullies didn't mean to beat you up. Let's go home."

The young Snark siblings walked through Wintersmells, with Bland and the Pink-Eyed Raven following behind them. As they approached the Wintersmells Public Library, they saw a chubby, bespectacled youth stroll out of the building, eating a powdered donut with one hand and stroking his neckbeard with the other. He excitedly waved when he noticed the Snarks.

"Is that—is that *Holdthedoorthezombosarecoming*?!" said Bland.

"Yes, that's him," said the Raven. "But as a child he went by a *different name…*"

"Greetings, friends!" the chubby boy said with a faux British accent.

"Hey, Ratpiss," said Deaddard.

The three children walked together, though adults were constantly stopping them to say hello to Ratpiss. He had just won the Wintersmells spelling bee for the fourth year in a row and was widely expected to announce his candidacy for mayor in the coming days. "My apologies, chaps," he chuckled to the Snarks amid the commotion. "Shall'st we duck into this alleyway for a moment of calm? There's something I'd like to show you."

Bland stared at Ratpiss in awe. He wondered how in the freakin' heck this charming, articulate young man had matured into an oaf who thought rocks were candy. He also wondered how much longer the Pink-Eyed Raven would make him watch this, since all in all it wasn't really *that* interesting. He saw the Raven pull a box of raisins from his pocket and pop a few in his mouth.

"No. Bring your own next time," the Raven croaked when Bland asked if he could have some. In defiance, Bland snatched a tasty-looking sandwich from a window sill and gobbled it down as he followed the children into a deserted alley.

Once there, Ratpiss took off his glasses and dropped the British accent. "Alright losers, let's do some drugs."

"I knew you were gonna make us do this," Deaddard sighed. "You're always such a kiss-up to adults and always so mean to us."

"Ooh, wah wah wah," said Ratpiss. "Wah wah, are you gonna cry? Are you gonna cry like a little baby? Wah? 'Cause of the little drug?"

"No!" said Deaddard, seconds away from crying. Ratpiss spat on his shoes.

Bland rolled his eyes and turned to the Pink-Eyed Raven. "Is this just some dumb morality lesson about how doing drugs will turn me stupid like Holdthedoor-thezombosarecoming?"

"Perhaps," the Raven said cryptically and clearly unsure.

Ratpiss pulled a large glass bottle out of his coat pocket. "It's *milk of the heroin*. Stole it from my mom's medicine cabinet." He took a pull from the bottle and slunk back against the wall as a doofy grin spread across his face.

Yomomma took the bottle from Ratpiss's flopping hand and examined it. "Does it feel . . . good?" she asked.

"It'll make you believe in God," Ratpiss slurred. "Here, hit this shit."

Deaddard squirmed uncomfortably. "I don't know about this, you guys. Isn't this stuff, like, really addictive?"

"Whoa, Deaddard, you gotta try this," said Yomomma, stretching her limbs in ecstasy.

Lacking both the morals and the social skills to correctly navigate this situation, Deaddard quickly gave in to the peer pressure and took a swig. His anxieties immediately disappeared, and he soon found himself reaching for the bottle again. Within minutes they had drained half the bottle, and the three of them sat in complete silence for a while, their eyes glazed over and emotionless.

"So why are you showing this to me?" Bland eventually asked the Pink-Eyed Raven.

"Yeah, this got pretty weird," he said. "I just wanted you to see that your dad was a huge dweeb. Let's go back."

They exited the vision and returned to reality. Bland breathed a sigh of relief and wheeled himself through the red curtain and onto the stage but accidentally ran over Fozzie Bear's foot in the process. Confused, he tried to turn around, but Fozzie's yelp of pain was misheard by Animal as the cue to detonate the large ring of dynamite that surrounded them. Bland frantically looked to the Pink-Eyed Raven for help but saw that he had *just* been tricked into five separate Chinese finger traps by the Swedish Chef.

"*What in the seven hells did you do*?!" the Pink-Eyed Raven screamed at Bland.

"I didn't do anything! Who are these guys?!" he screamed back.

"You clearly altered something in the past and caused a butterfly effect, you stupid idiot!"

"Quiet on the set, everyone!" said Kermit. "The show is about to begin!" Everybody scrambled to get to their places.

"You didn't tell me that could happen!" Bland shouted over Dr. Teeth warming up the band. "All I did was grab a sandwich!"

"Well, you better go find another sandwich and put it back!"

"We better find a better book and get our money back!" said Statler to Waldorf.

Trying to escape the commotion, Bland accidentally flipped his wheelchair over a clucking chicken and fell face first into a custard pie. With the strength of his massive arms, he threw himself down the nearest staircase and dragged his body around until he miraculously found a catering table.

"Has anyone seen my $9,000 custard pie?" asked Miss Piggy.

He spotted Gonzo preparing to take a bite out of the last sandwich in the food display. *Ah*, Gonzo happily sighed to himself. *I finally have a free moment to enjoy my delicious sandwich in peace and quiet.*

Bland swiftly yanked it from his hands and wanked back to Wintersmells. Everything was as it should have been: the town smelled like shit, the kids were still strung out, and all was quiet in the streets—until Donny Slick burst through a door swinging a battle axe. "If I don't find my sandwich in thirty seconds, *I'm gonna do something nuts*!" he kept screaming.

"Really makes you rethink history, huh?" the Pink-Eyed Raven said, appearing behind Bland. "Now put the dang sandwich back, and let's go."

"Oh, there it is," said Donny Slick after Bland put it on a table behind him. "Never mind everyone! Forget any of this happened." And everyone did.

With the universe restored to normal, the Pink-Eyed Raven announced that it was his bedtime. He had Bland apply magic antibacterial cream to his magic swollen eyes, as he did every night, and fell into a deep, noisy sleep. As Bland did his nightly one hundred crouching hover planks before bed, he tried to recount everything he had learned that day. If messing with the past had dire consequences for the present, then it would make sense that messing with the future would also have dire consequences but ultimately have no effect on him whatsoever. He decided the only thing to do would be to wank into the future, tell people he was a god, and see if any girls would find that attractive.

So as the Pink-Eyed Raven slept, snoring really loud and weird, Bland grabbed ahold of a weirdwood branch and wanked as hard as he could. He found himself standing at the top of a snowy hillside. A creaky voice spoke behind him.

"And now that we've raised the zombos from the dead, me and my army will march into Wintersmells and take over the world!"

Bland recognized the face from the decals on the punching bags at his gym. It was the Nighty Night King—the most dangerous terrorist in the world. And sure enough, in the valley below him were hundreds of thousands of zombos standing in formation.

"Ooh, Mr. Nighty Night, I can't wait for you to rule the whole wide world," said a tattered rag doll in the king's left hand.

"Yes, Penelope Peanut, we will finally play teatime in a real-life palace," said the king.

"And will there be ice cream every day?" asked Percival the Polar Bear in his right hand.

The king simply smiled, and the three best buddies kissed as the army of White Wieners and zombos stared ahead in obedient silence. Bland stifled a laugh. The king suddenly whipped around.

"Who's there?" he shouted. Bland stood frozen, still unsure whether the murky, inconsistent rules of the Pink-Eyed Raven's magic made him visible to the king or not. He tried to wank out of the vision but realized he didn't know how to do it without the Raven's help. The Nighty Night King delicately placed Penelope and Percival in their doll house and started slowly pacing around the hilltop. "Whoever's spying on me…they're not dolls, they're limited-edition action figures," he insisted.

Suddenly the king locked eyes with Bland and lunged at him. "Swear on your life you won't tell anyone!" he shouted, giving Bland an Indian burn on his arm. Bland struggled to break free, but the king's grip tightened more and more.

The world around him started to dissolve, and Bland soon found himself back in the cave, being shaken out of the vision by Scooby. The Nighty Night King was gone, but there was still a glowing blue mark on his arm where he had gotten the Indian burn. The Pink-Eyed Raven glared at him.

"You fool! Now that the Nighty Night King has touched you, the zombos will be able to cross the magic force field that was protecting this cave!"

"I don't really see how that makes any sense," said Bland.

"I dunno man, that's just the rules!" said the Pink-Eyed Raven, trembling with fear. "They're going to be here any minute. Leave while you can."

Bland grabbed ahold of a branch. "No, no, I can fix this," he said, and he wanked back to the future to make things right.

Except when he looked around he realized he was back in the alleyway with Deaddard, Yomomma, and Ratpiss passed out on the floor. "Goddammit," he said.

"Whoa, hey, are you a cop?" said Ratpiss, stirring to life.

"No, I'm..." Bland stalled while he tried to wank out of the vision, but the magic failed him once again. "I'm, uh, an ex-cop."

"Cool. You wanna hit this shit?" Ratpiss offered him the bottle of milk of the heroin. At this point, Bland figured the Pink-Eyed Raven would have a plan for dealing with the zombos and could probably transport him back to the cave if he needed him for anything. And even if his interacting with Ratpiss in the past caused another butterfly effect, maybe it would prevent the Nighty Night King from entering the cave. It seemed like he had nothing to lose.

"What's the butterfly effect?" asked Ratpiss.

"Wow, this is really strong shit," said Bland, taking another pull from the bottle.

Meanwhile, the army of zombos had reached the Pink-Eyed Raven's cave. They breezed through the magic force field and started banging on the cave's front door. "Let us in!" they said in their zombo language.

The Pink-Eyed Raven nudged Bland's crumpled up body with his branch. "Bland! Come out of your vision! The zombos are coming!" But no response. Scooby tried gnawing at his legs but remembered Bland had lost all feeling in them long ago. He tried gnawing at Bland's arms, but his mouth couldn't fit around the massive circumference of his muscles. Bland was out cold.

"The hell is wrong with you, Bland?! You need to get out of here!" the Raven screamed. Despite the commotion, Holdthedoorthezombosarecoming had gotten stuck in a bear trap a few hours earlier and had fallen asleep there. "Wake up, wake up, wake up!"

Bland vaguely heard something in the distance but quickly decided it wasn't important. He took another swig, fist-pumped the air, and put his arm around his young father. "You wanna know about the future?" he slurred. "Let's just say, they're not making a sequel to *Avatar…they're making five.*" Deaddard's eyes widened. "Unbelievable," he said.

"Unfuckingbelievable," cried the Pink-Eyed Raven, peering into Bland's vision. But before he could pull him out of it, one of the zombos suddenly punched his fist through the door of the cave.

"Oh fuck," said the Pink-Eyed Raven.

"Zoinks!" said Scooby.

"Holdthedoorthezombosarecoming!" screamed the Raven, returning to the cave. "Wake up! We need you to hold the door because the zombos are coming!"

Holdthedoorthezombosarecoming rubbed his eyes open and stared blankly at the Raven. He pointed to the ceiling.

"Holdthedoorthezombosarecoming?" he said slowly.

"No, you idiot! Hold *the door*! The zombos are coming!"

Holdthedoorthezombosarecoming chewed on his index finger for a bit, then quickly nodded his head in understanding. He started picking up handfuls of dirt from the floor and stuffing as much as he could into his pockets. "Holdthedoorthezombosarecoming," he grunted.

"That's not it at all!!" screamed the Pink-Eyed Raven.

At this point, Bland could no longer ignore the distant yelling. He assumed it was the Pink-Eyed Raven going on about something, but he couldn't quite make out what he was saying. "Sorry, guys, I think someone's trying to tell me something," he told his friends as he tried to get closer to the sound.

"All good, my man," said Ratpiss. "I should get going anyway. I just remembered I was supposed to pick up my grandma's prize-winning ant farm from the vet today."

"Do you not see the zombos coming through that door?! Put down my fucking umbrella! We do not need that!" Bland heard the Raven's faraway voice say.

"You have to enunciate, Raven!" Bland yelled at the sky. "Is everything okay up there?"

"What is wrong with you? Hold the door, the zombos are coming!"

"Wank into young Holdthedoorthezombosarecoming?" Bland thought he heard him say. "Well, okay. If you say so."

With his amateur magic skills, Bland wanked into Ratpiss's mind just as he was leaving the vet with his grandma's prize-winning ant farm. Obviously he did it incorrectly, and Ratpiss began to violently seize. His eyes rolled back into his head as the ant farm shattered completely and millions of angry fire ants swarmed his body.

"Hold the door the zombos are coming!" Ratpiss screamed, reflexively echoing the Pink-Eyed Raven's constant shouting. "Hold the door the zombos are coming!"

This feels incorrect, thought Bland. *I wonder why the Pink-Eyed Raven wanted me to do that.*

Ratpiss continued writhing on the floor. "Hold thedoorthe zombos arecoming," he stammered, impulsively trying to fit his fist inside his belly button. By now a ring of townspeople had formed around him, and people were starting to get concerned.

"My son!" screamed his mother, running up to the scene.

"My ants!" screamed his grandmother.

"Holdthedoorthezombosarecoming! Holdthedoorthe-zombosarecoming! Holdthedoorthezombosarecoming!" he chanted as he spun in circles on the floor, suddenly seeming to enjoy himself.

"Oh my god," Bland said. "This whole time . . . 'Hold-thedoorthezombosarecoming' actually meant 'Hold the door the zombos are coming!' I gotta tell Scoob!"

With this new burst of motivation, Bland passed the magic threshold necessary to wank himself out of the vision and back to the cave. He came back to life in his wheel-chair, as the Pink-Eyed Raven was half-assedly slapping him across the face with his branches to wake him up. Now that he understood his life's purpose, Holdthedoorthezombos-arecoming was struggling with all his might to hold the cave door shut, because the zombos were coming. And he was losing the battle.

"We're all screwed, kid," said the Pink-Eyed Raven with a hoarse voice. "If we're being honest, you're prob-ably the least talented wank I've ever seen. But you must leave here now and return to Wintersmells. Your family needs you to use your training."

Bland gave the Raven's tree branch a firm handshake. "Thank you for everything. If we're being honest, your training was completely useless—" Just then, the door broke down and hordes of zombos flooded in.

"But *this* is what I've been training for."

Bland did a double back handspring out of his wheel-chair and took off running on his hands. As the zombos tore Scooby and Holdthedoorthezombosarecoming limb from limb, and as the Nighty Night King triumphantly chopped down the Pink-Eyed Raven's weirdwood tree, Bland began the two-hundred-mile trek back to Winter-smells, his weak legs continuously flopping in his face.

"Wocka wocka!" said Fozzie Bear, taking in the destruction.

Dennys

They say that when a Grandslam is born, the Gods flip a dragon to see if they get a coin or not. And when Dennys Grandslam was born, her coin had landed on the angriest dragon of them all. *That settles it*, thought the hotheaded Dragon Queen. *No one is coming to save me. Not Yora Mormon, not Beerion, not my dragons, and not the unappreciative former slaves I freed back in Submeereen.* She would have to take matters into her own hotheaded hands.

Dennys had been captured by the Clothkhaki and made captive in their inimitable holy city, Vegas Clothkhak. Years ago they'd considered her their very own cholesteroleesi, but now they only considered her to be a former cholesteroleesi at best. Would they toss her in with the rest of the former cholesteroleesis in the straw hut where they were forced to knit for the remainder of their lives? Or would they sell her into slavery and use the profits to buy fine knitted goods? "Maybe they'll chalk all this up to a big hilarious misunderstanding," said Dennys optimistically. "And then they'll set me free so I can return to Submeereen to fight off the rebellious slavers who besieged the city? Yes, yes. A misunderstanding."

"Miss, understand this: stop talking! Your voice sounds like nails on a chalkboard." A man wearing mostly rags, with a few accents of smeared poop here and there, accosted Dennys from the corner of the cell.

"Is that so? And who might *you* be? What are *you* in for?" Dennys was taken aback by the man's imaginative insult.

"Name's Tony. I ain't did nothing. I just like to sleep in these cells and pretend I'm still a prisoner like back in the golden years before they pardoned me. Three square meals a week and a wet bed to sleep on. Boy, what a way to spend my thirties." Tony's eyes twinkled at the fond memory.

Suddenly a muscular bearded man came to the cell's bars and unlocked the door. Taunting Dennys he said, "Cholesteroleesi, it is time for your trial. Follow me to the—Tony. Man, we have talked about this. Tony, you cannot stay here anymore."

"Aye aye, cap'n. See you tomorrow, same time!" Tony skipped away.

"No, Tony. Don't come back. What don't you understand? Damn, he's gone. Alright, Dennys, let's go. Now we're late."

Dennys stood in front of the central temple, summoned by the Clothkhaki leaders to decide her fate. She entered, armed with nothing except courage in her heart and a shank in her hand in case she needed it.

"I didn't realize the ugly convention was in town," said one of the leaders in the Clothkhaki language upon seeing Dennys. "Let's sell this ugly uggo to the slavers."

"No!" protested another man in the same tongue. "I like ugly girls. Let's keep her."

These clowns don't realize I speak their language, thought Dennys, trying very hard to remind herself that the Clothkhaki hold different cultural beauty ideals than Westopolians.

"Gentlemen, behave yourselves," spoke Cholesterol Bonor, leader of the Clothkhaki, still using their native tongue. "Obviously we all agree she's ugly. But she belongs with the rest of the widows of our past cholesterols: in the straw hut where we lock them all up."

Time to reveal I've understood them all along, thought Dennys.

"Don't you want to know where bathroom sand gallops for horse lunchtime?" she proclaimed, her Clothkhaki pretty rusty after all these years. Dennys stood confidently, positive that she had just elegantly asked if they would let her plead her case through an impassioned speech.

The confused men stared at her. "What?"

With the help of a translator they brought in, Dennys was able to ask the men for a chance to give her speech.

"And the only prop I'll need for my speech," she said, "is a lit torch."

"We don't allow fire within the city," Cholesterol Bonor replied. "This is sacred ground."

"Well, I need it for the speech."

"Hmm. Does the speech use fire as an important central metaphor?" he asked.

"Umm...yes?"

"Okay, fine," he said as he handed her a broad, fiery stick, and with that, Dennys began.

"Gentlemen, what does it mean to be Clothkhaki? Allow me to improvise for a moment to distract you fine sirs. Why don't I start a fire right now?" Dennys threw the torch against the temple's soft straw walls, setting the hut ablaze. The fire spread quickly, engulfing the dry temple completely in mere seconds. The men sprinted for the door, but Dennys had locked it shut with thick bars of straw before entering. The entire hut went up in flames. Fortunately for Dennys, she was impervious to fire.

"You fool," said the Clothkhaki, in unison. "We are fireproof as well." Unfortunately for Dennys, this was true. She found out that most people were, in fact, generally unharmed by fire and that she was not really all that special.

I have failed, she thought. *I suppose there's always... Plan B.* But before she could start shanking people, she noticed the heads of the scorched men and realized maybe she hadn't failed after all.

"Your hair has all burned off," she said, addressing the newly bald leaders collectively. "And because of the dumb Clothkhaki rules that you all abide by, that means you've been completely emasculated and aren't in charge anymore." She shook her glorious silver hair back and forth, emitting a huge cloud of dandruff. "Everyone here knows that the person with the longest hair is in charge, and it looks like that just became me."

The men patted their bald heads frantically, realizing Dennys was now in charge.

"But . . . but . . . how? Your hair? It didn't burn?" trembled Cholesterol Bonor.

"She's a witch! Burn the witch!" shouted one of the men.

After several minutes of futilely trying to burn Dennys's fireproof Grandslam hair, the men solemnly gave up.

"This woman is our new leader," said former cholesterol Bonor holding Dennys's indestructible hair. "And if you have a problem with that, you'll have to go through me!"

The men were silent for a moment.

"And me!" shouted another.

"Hold on now. I loved Dennys from the very beginning. I just did not want to seem overtly contrarian in front of the fellas, you know?" said the meanest-looking man.

"Excuse me, I love Dennys, and I will die for her. Is that okay with everyone?"

"Would you guys mind stepping back so I can have a direct line of sight to Dennys? *My* cholesteroleesi!"

Dennys commanded them to bring an army to Submeereen, and they enthusiastically agreed, following her out of their ancient, holy, historically important city as it burned down behind them.

∼≽⊱∼

In an effort to retake the city, the former slavers had launched a siege from Submeereen's bay, Forced Labor Lagoon. Dennys charged into battle outside Submeereen's walls with a Clothkhaki horde at her back and quickly retreated, letting them deal with it instead.

While the Clothkhaki fought for her, Dennys ran to the palace, where she found Beerion rolling around giddily with a pint in hand, just as she had left him.

"Dennsyyss!" slurred her tiny advisor. Beerion began their secret handshake. He jumped as high as he could to high-five her, only reaching her kneecap, and landed inside her shoe. He giggled while snuggling up inside her shoe as the city walls were bombarded with flaming debris. "Did you know Dog Shit and Ms. Andei are a thing? You know, Dog Shit, he, you know, Dog Shit doesn't have a butthole? Hahahaha. Those poor bastards, the Funsullied. Come let us drink to their buttless honor!" Beerion gulped down an ale and kicked his feet jovially.

"Beerion, for your valor during my captivity and continued devotion, I now promote you to Best Man of the Queen. Congratulations."

"And I pronounce ayoo-hoo too sober! Come have a drink to celebrate my promotion!" shouted Beerion, throwing back a glass of ale.

41

Dennys politely shook her head in disgust and handed Beerion his new Best Man pin. He immediately collapsed under the immense weight of the four-ounce pin that was twice the size of his torso. Behind him, Dennys caught the eye of an old friend.

"Hello, Dennys, it is I, your very young friend!" Yora Mormon wheezed out. "Thank the Gods you're back! I would've just killed myself if you'd died with the Cloth-khaki. My sweet precious queen being killed? Okay, life over. No point in living anymore." He adjusted the three-inch-thick lenses on his glasses. "By the way, check out my fresh new shoes! They're sneakers. Pretty fly, huh? That's what all the cool kids are wearing these days. Lord Varysectomy told me about them. They'll be really dope with my skateboard. Oh, damn, I forgot my skateboard. I can't show you any tricks now." Yora took a huge breath from his inhaler and adjusted the orthopedic inserts in his shoes.

"Hey Yora…" said Dennys, trying to think of an excuse not to have to talk to him.

"Your Grace! I heard you were back and came running at once," Dog Shit cried, entering the palace's court-yard. "We must go meet with the commanding enemy slavers."

Thank the Gods, thought Dennys. "Yora, I can't talk anymore because I have an excuse. Hello, Dog Shit!"

"Fuck you, Dog Shit," Beerion said, tossing him a gold coin and kicking his shin. "Go buy yourself a butt." Beer-ion tried to high-five Dennys but missed and fell over.

Dog Shit took Dennys and Beerion to meet with the enemy commanders on a plateau overlooking the city and Forced Labor Lagoon. The three slavers wore ornate short swords at their belt, but this meeting, they all hoped, would remain peaceful. The fighting had come to a temporary standstill.

"You stand before Dennys Grandslam," announced Dog Shit to the slavers, "Rightful Queen of the Sandals and the Thirsty Men. Fan of the Chicken Tenders and Mother of Draggin, Dragun, and Jragon."

"Surrender now and I'll let you all live," announced Dennys.

"Oh? But it is *you* who will be surrendering, Mrs. Dragon Queen. We've got your city surrounded."

"Oh? Oh?" said Dennys. "But actually, it is actually you—the person who will be doing the surrendering of cities, that is," retorted Dennys clumsily.

"No deal," said the slavers as they began to walk away.

But Dennys had one trick up her sleeve that she hadn't used yet. "Maybe *this* will change your mind," she said, whistling as loud as she could. The whistle was a signal. Beerion knew what to do—he emptied his pockets and let all the coins spill onto the ground. "A few golds each? Huh? Sweeten the deal?" she asked.

But it wasn't enough to persuade the slavers. They continued on their way out.

"They're getting away!" pleaded Dog Shit.

"Ah fine," said Dennys. "I'll do the dragon thing. It just feels like it's my gimmick at this point." Dennys stomped down her foot. "*Gasolina*!" she shouted in the high Ovarian tongue.

Draggin, Dragun, and Jragon came bounding out into the sky, exploring the open air for the first time in months. They were going stir-crazy locked up in the basement and happily leapt into action immediately, tossing and turning about, flipping and cannonballing, completing ignoring the enemy ships.

"Hey! Dragons! Go after the ships! *Gasolina*! That means 'shoot fire,' you idiots! *Gasolina*!" Dennys was steamed. But the dragons didn't care. They were having a rip-roaring good time playing in the sky and water. As the dragons decked each other midair and wrestled around above the seas, suddenly it became clear that it wasn't just harmless fun and games. The dragons were roughhousing so hard that they were accidentally landing on enemy ships.

"No, no, no!" shouted the slavers, as Draggin gave his brother Jragon a wet willy that caused him to freak out and fly straight through a warship's hull. Upset that he was being left out of the play fighting, Dragun threw a tantrum by eating an entire crew off another warship. The slavers were in awe of the mighty dragons.

"Enough," said the slavers. "Enough! Call off your vicious beasts! We surrender!"

"I accept your surrender," said Dennys. She continued after a moment, "But you must choose one among the three of you to die, as a punishment for your crimes."

"Pick me," said one of the men. "I am lowborn. I insist you pick me."

"No, it should be me," said another of the three. "You two are the best guys I know."

"I couldn't live to watch either of you die," asserted the last man. "It must be me."

"I said...pick me!"

"No one is dying except me!"

"Let me do this!"

Before long, the argument had turned into a fist fight. "So that's how it's going to be, eh?" shouted one of them, drawing his short sword and slitting his own throat. "See! Already did it. Too late for you!"

"Nope!" said the other, slitting his own throat. "Just cut my throat even deeper. I'm going to die first. Bandage yourself up."

The last man stepped forward. "Not if I die first," he said, shoving his sword right through his head and flopping forward.

"Dammit!" shouted the other two before they too flopped forward and died.

And so, on that mountaintop the three slavers killed each other. Dennys freed the slaves and commandeered their ships, finally setting sail for Westopolis with a horde of Clothkhaki, legions of Funsullied, three dragons, and one extraordinarily tiny Best Man. All was right with the world. The end of the book. Or is it? Keep reading to find out.

Cervix

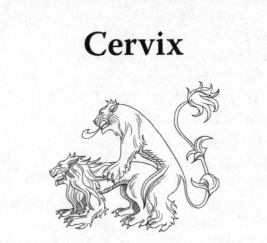

The trial of the Queen Mommy Cervix Bangsister was about to begin. Cervix had two choices before her: confess to her sins and get a bird carved into her forehead by a Gods-loving twelve-year-old with a knife or refuse to confess and get stabbed to death by a Gods-loving twelve-year-old with a knife.

Thousands had packed themselves into the Newly Fire-Resistant Sept of the Latter Day Saints to see what the least beloved woman in all of Westopolis would choose. There was just one small problem. Cervix Bangsister was nowhere to be found.

"I found her!" shouted one of the newest Beaky Buzzards from the upper decks of the Sept. "Wait, no I didn't. Sorry about that, folks."

His Beakiness scratched the part of his forehead where all of his followers had scars carved in the shape of birds.

(He didn't have the scar because, as he had explained hundreds of times, "I uh, um, I just don't need it, and I'm closer to the Gods than the rest of the Beaky Buzzards, and I do a lot for the organization, so I don't need a bird scar on my forehead.") "Where in the seven hells is Cervix Bangsister?"

Cervix looked out at the Sept from the window of her room in the Red Queef and gulped down her third goblet of wine that month. It was the morning of July 1 and a fine morning it was, but certainly made more fine with wine. She needed to stay sharp on such a momentous day. She poured herself the fourth and final goblet of wine she'd allow herself to drink until the top of the hour. *Caaannn't get tooooo drunnnnkk*, she thought. *I wannna, um, gotta remmemember what it's gonnnna look like when my enemies, as well as a bunnnch of raaaanndom civillians perish innnn a fiery essplooosion.*

Again and again Cervix thought about the mistake that had led her here: she'd had incest with the wrong family member. Usually she had a great sense of which family members were perfectly fine to take to the bedroom, with few, if any, repercussions. Imma Bangsister (nephew), Trynna Bangsister (nephew), Luvtue Bangsister (great-uncle), Hopentue Bangsister (nephew), Ineeda Bangsister (nephew), Iwanna Bangsister (nephew), Fuckbrother Bangsister (nephew), Igotta Bangsister (no relation). All of them had been inside the once queen of Westopolis. These seven boys and one man were handpicked for incest by Cervix, and no one who mattered cared.

Even back when she was queen, Cervix would have sex with her twin brother Lemme almost every night. In fact, even back when she was a child, Cervix would try to convince Lemme that it was okay for them to be having sex almost every night and then would proceed to have sex with Lemme on most of those nights.

And how did that end up for Lemme? He'd gotten one of the most important parts of his body cut right off: his head. Gone, just like that. Now he wore a prosthetic gold head like some kind of a freak.

"Incest gave me my son Jeffy and my son Timid," said Cervix out loud to no one. "And it gave me the daughter that I have too, who has a name that I can't remember right now. She's…somewhere." Cervix sat on her bed pensively, continuing to rationalize her choices to herself out loud. "Maybe King Jeffy had three hands and no mouth, but was that an incest thing? Probably not? And look at Timid. King Timid Boaratheon, my beautiful, beautiful hot baby boy. My lovely, kind, sexually attractive son. Did incest mess him up? Huh? Did it? It's very possible, so did it? Have I birthed a defective child once again? Have we yet to observe the ways in which incest has messed up my hot baby son?"

What does it matter, she thought. *For once incest has messed* me *up*. Her mistake: Incel Bangsister, her thirteen-year-old cousin. *I'd still be having consequence-free incest as often as I liked if not for that little bitch*. As soon as Incel joined the Beaky Buzzards, he snitched on Cervix, like a little bitch. As one of the fanatic religious cult's newest members, he would devote his life thereafter to the Seven Gods: the Father, the Mother, the Hamburglar, Officer Big Mac, Mayor McCheese, Grimace, the Chicken McNuggmonster, Dr. McFlurry, French Fry and the Ketchup Kids, Auntie Cheese, and the rest.

The Beaky Buzzards had taken over King's Landing Strip with their army of surprisingly fit young boys almost overnight. Citizens of the Strip used to only participate in the fun parts of religion, like believing in the Heavens, marrying minors, and Halloween. Now the Buzzards made sure everyone partook in the not-fun parts too, like believing in the seven hells and it being mandatory to get stabbed in the forehead.

And now they had broken the camel's back with a piece of straw. Is that—? That doesn't sound right...Regardless, Cervix was to stand trial. Except she wasn't actually going to stand trial. She was going to sit. Sit in her room, that is. Sit in her room while orphan children blew it up. Blew up the Sept, specifically. Blew it up with mildfire, precisely. Mildfire, exactly, to blow up all the Beaky Buzzards so she wouldn't have to go to trial. Blow them up, of course, so they'd die, that is. Cervix grinned and reached for another goblet of wine.

Back in the Sept, His Beakiness stood at the center of a crowd that grew more and more frustrated with Cervix's absence.

"All a part of the Gods' plan," he calmly stated.

"Don't you see?" urged Manmeat Thighspell, the queen of Westopolis. "Cervix is not here. My mother-in-law knows how severe the consequences are for missing her trial and yet she still did not appear. Something feels off. We all need to leave. Now."

Back in the Red Queef, King Timid Boaratheon put his cute little crown on his cute little head and looked at himself in the mirror.

"Tonight's the night I ask Queen Manmeat to let me try anal," he proclaimed. "And tonight's the night she says yes, maybe."

Timid closed his eyes and strutted toward the door singing an impromptu song: "I'm gonna put my wiener in a butt, uh huh, and sex is my favorite thing, oh yeah. Now off to this trial to make my wife happy; I think my mom might die—" But Timid stopped singing and opened his eyes when he ran face first into a Kingsguardsman.

"Ouch!" yelped the tiny king, rubbing his forehead where he bonked it on the soldier's armor. "Excuse me, but I've got to get to the trial." The man wouldn't move. "You're blocking the doorway, which prevents me from being able to leave the building and go to the trial." The guardsman held position, completely silent. "Oh, wait," realized Timid. "I'm the king. I command you to move, please." No dice. The soldier held strong. "Or, um, uhh, um"—Timid had one last plan—"I guess I could just hang out in my room for the rest of the day?" Timid took off his crown and went back to jumping on his bed.

Tension was building in the Sept. Queen Manmeat was frantic. "I literally just shit myself, everybody," she proclaimed. It was a lie. "I swear to the Gods, I just shit in my clothes!" She hadn't defecated in weeks. "That's how scared I am. We need to leave right now or we're going to die."

"Believe it or not," announced His Beakiness, while smelling the queen's rear end and making a face to communicate that everything down there smelled normal and the queen was lying, "I understand where Queen Manmeat is coming from. At this point, it seems pretty likely that Cervix Bangsister is planning some sort of attack on us, perhaps in the form of an explosion that will kill us all and stop her from receiving her punishment. But to you I say this: I don't *care*. 'Tis the Gods' plan. If we die in an explosion? I do not care. Any one of you could come down here right now and beat the shit out of me, and I would not care. Wanna fuck my wife? The Gods' plan. You wanna kill me and have sex with my dead body? That's awesome. Allow me to assist you. At the end of the day—"

Cervix woke up when she heard the *BOOM bang BOOM owww help me! For the love of the Gods! The building is going down we're all gonna die KABOOM* of the Newly Fire-Resistant Sept of the Latter Day Saints exploding. *Oh no no no no no no no no no*, Cervix thought as she rushed to get out of bed. *Shit shit shit shit shit. Please no. Please no.* She hurried to her window and looked at the rubble where the Sept used to be. *Awwwww, come on! I missed the entire explosion like an idiot?* The sky was red with the ashes of the Sept, the Beaky Buzzards, His Beakiness, and the rest of Cervix's enemies in the Strip.

A nap? I thought a nap was a good idea? I knew the Sept was set to blow in five minutes and I laid down to take a quick nap?

Cervix planted the palm of her hand into her face. *I guess alcohol and mildfire do not mix well*, she thought, chuckling to herself and pouring some mildfire into her wine to see how it would taste. *Not bad.*

⚜

Smoke filled the air all throughout the Red Queef. The nightmarish sounds of hacking coughs echoed through the dusty, ash-covered castle walls as they did everywhere else in the city. One could not walk outside without getting a face full of human ash. Every citizen of the Strip (no matter how rich or how poor) would almost certainly contract a respiratory ailment shortly. Cervix had never been so happy. Such a glorious success called for a bottle of wine to celebrate. She even got a second bottle so that Timid could have some.

"I don't want wine," complained the immature boy. "I want Queen Manmeat." Even for a twelve-year-old, he was acting like a childish, sober baby.

"Timid, you just have to trust me on this. You're really overreacting right now," explained his mother. Cervix pondered for a moment. *Why is he being so annoying about this?* Then, it came to her. "Is it intercourse, my son? Is that what this is about? Would you like to go to bed with mother?"

"I *don't* want to have sex with you, mother!" cried out the melodramatic king. "What will my friends think?

That I can't have sex with a regular girl like Manmeat? Well, it's not true! I can have sex all by myself!"

How do I get him to shut up? Cervix calculated. "My son, maybe Manmeat isn't even dead. For all we know, she actually survived that massive explosion." She could not help but snicker at the preposterousness of the thought.

"You're Gods damned right I did." It was Queen of Westopolis Manmeat Thighspell. Alive as ever, standing in the doorway, spinning a plate on her finger.

"Sexwife!" exclaimed King Timid. "I mean, Manmeat!" he said, correcting himself, moving a heavy book onto his lap. "You didn't get dead!"

Fuck, thought Cervix. "Manmeat. You...are alive. This is...news. I'm so..." Cervix was so enraged that she could not remember the word "happy." *Shit, shit, shit. Come on, Cervix. What's the word for "not sad"? Slippery? Candle? Slippery?* "Heppy." *Yes, that's it.*

"I'm the only person who survived the explosion," explained Manmeat, ripping off all her clothes and doing a 360-degree twirl, "but it came at a price." The beautiful queen stood naked, unscathed by the explosion save for one complication. Both of her private parts (front and back) had been 100 percent seared shut for good by the fire.

"Oh," eked out the young Timid, pale as a ghost. "I suppose...this means we can't have sex anymore?"

"It would be impossible, Your Grace," replied Queen Manmeat in a somber tone.

"I see," said the boy. And so, King Timid Boaratheon, First of His Friends to Touch a Boob, Sitter on the Pointy Chair, Person in Charge of Westopolis, then removed the heavy book from his lap, stood up, and calmly launched himself out the fifteenth-story window to his death.

❧

The Chair Room was filled to the brim with truly random citizens grabbed off the streets. Sideburn, the maester to the crown and Cervix Bangsister's personal mad scientist, popped out from a secret panel in the floor giggling a maniacal laugh.

"Gods, how long have you been hiding down there, Sideburn?" whispered Cervix. "You smell disgusting."

Sideburn cleared his throat. "I now proclaim Cervix of the House Bangsister, fifteenth of her name, Queen of the Sandals and Thirsty Men, Protector of the Chair, Person in Charge of Westopolis."

He held up the tiara he'd forged the previous night. He smiled, admiring his handiwork, then put away the tiara and unveiled Cervix's new crown. "All hail Queen Cervix," he said, placing the crown on her head with one hand and discreetly rubbing the tiara against his groin with the other.

The new queen stood on the Pointy Chair. "My Queen," whispered Sideburn. "The chair is for sitting. You must sit in the chair."

"I see," said Cervix, squatting in place on top of the Pointy Chair. The citizens of Westopolis gave her a standing ovation as she held the squat for nearly thirty seconds. *I'm queen alright*, thought Cervix, massaging her tired quadriceps.

When the crowning ceremony was finished, Sideburn took Queen Cervix down to his laboratory in the cellars of the Red Queef. "Have you ever been down here before, Your Grace?" asked Sideburn.

"Obviously not," replied the queen, holding her nose closed. "Oof. Sideburn, I'm serious. What is that horrible smell?"

Sideburn giggled. "I'll never tell."

I truly may vomit, so this ought to be good, thought the queen.

"Queen Cervix, I've brought you down here to show you something that, in a word, ought to be good. Your Grace, when I heard that one of the Grandslam girl's dragons was slightly wounded while fighting in Submeereen, I was so overwhelmed that I cried for four days. Just crying and crying and crying, couldn't be stopped. I really don't know if I am okay psychologically. You see, if dragons can be wounded, then dragons can be injured. And if they can be injured, then they can be hurt. So, I've developed a weapon that can hurt a dragon so bad that it actually dies."

"This is fantastic news, Sideburn," said Cervix. "Is that the weapon right there?" she asked, pointing at what appeared to be a pile of dog corpses.

"That's nothing," answered Sideburn quickly. "Don't worry about that." He nudged the pile of dogs into a corner with his foot. "The finest blacksmiths and artisans in all the Strip have been laboring day and night on this, Your Grace. It's nothing short of a leap forward in human ingenuity and creativity." He yanked away a giant cloth, revealing the weapon: a gigantic, massive sword. "It takes thirty men to just to hold this thing," said Sideburn proudly. "Takes fifty to swing it."

"So this will work? This will wound her dragons?" asked the queen with excitement.

"No," replied the maester. "It's more likely that it will just kill them."

Clink. Clink. Clink. went the footsteps of a juggernaut of a behemoth of a really big man approaching from the darkness. "Ah, yes," said Sideburn. "Your Grace, I have the honor of introducing you to the newest member of the Kingsguard, err, Queensguard, err, no, that doesn't sound good. I'm just going to say Kingsguard because I want to." Cervix looked up at the man. He stood at least nine feet tall. He was as wide as three men but not in a fat way. He was covered in armor head to toe and was dead silent. "You remember Ser Greggy, of course," said Sideburn.

"Nope," said Cervix.

"The Building?" asked the maester.

"The Building!" Cervix smiled fondly. "Why didn't you just say it was the Building in the first place? I'd never forget such an ugly, disfigured freak as the Building. I thought he was dead."

"He was," said Sideburn. "But now...he still is basically. That doesn't matter. If it please Your Grace, Ser

Greggy has taken a holy vow of silence. He has sworn that he will not speak until all of Your Grace's enemies are dead and evil has been driven from the realm."

"Is this true?" asked Cervix.

"Yes," replied Ser Greggy.

"Is this arrangement to your liking, Your Grace?" asked Sideburn.

Yes, thought Cervix Bangsister. *Oh, yes.*

"Sorry, is that a yes? You're just looking at him and smiling completely silently. I can get rid of Ser Greggy if you want," said Sideburn.

"No, yes. Yes," said Cervix.

"No, yes, yes?" asked Sideburn, confused and frustrated. "Is it 'no' or 'yes' or 'yes'?"

"It's yes, Sideburn," said Cervix, looking at her massive new bodyguard. "It's yes."

Malarya

Malarya Snark awoke in her bed, the sidewalk. She had been roaming the streets of Blahblahblahvos for months, tricking people into thinking she was a beggar by asking for money and starving to death. In addition to this she had to deal with the loss of her vision, which wasn't all that bad, except people constantly berated her and beat her up because her eyes were a little milky looking and were hanging out of their sockets. This turned out to be a positive as she then learned a new type of fighting—fighting the adversities faced by millions of visually disabled people every day.

All this was part of Malarya's training with the Tasteless Men, a secret order of Blahblahblahvosi assassins who disguised themselves by wearing dead people's bloody faces. Malarya had sought them out to learn the art of killing people really hard, so she could ultimately eliminate everyone on her kill list. Malarya recited the list aloud: "Walty Fuck. Cervix Bangsister. Um . . ." She found herself struggling before she even got to the hard part of the list, which had two guys in a row named "Throwup Jackson" whom she could never tell apart. "Uhhhh . . . Cervix Bangsister . . . Ed Sheeran?" *That can't be right*, she thought. *Ed Sheeran? The genre-redefining singer-songwriter-guitarist?* Malarya would have to take her own word for it.

Malarya had been in Blahblahblahvos for far too long. She wanted desperately to be back in Westopolis—she hadn't seen her remaining family in years, and she felt unwelcome in this strange land. She had no allies here, no friends, and the people of Blahblahblahvos would never accept her as anything more than a foreigner. Plus the public transit was garbage, and you ended up having to horse everywhere. But it was still too early in her training—she hadn't been given a single target to assassinate.

Malarya heard a coin drop into the small collection box she had in front of her. "It has been too long, girl," said a man's voice. Malarya recognized the voice—it was Jaqof Cigar, her mentor, one of the Tasteless Men. He came at the top of every hour to kick over Malarya's collection box and make fun of her goofy eyes.

"Please, Jaqof, don't—"

"After six months in the streets, has a girl finally become no one?"

"What does that mean?"

"Would someone who is no one ask questions?"

"You just did."

"I'm not no one. I'm Jaqof."

"Well, then, I don't want to be no one."

"Well, you have to be no one, so—"

"I'm Malarya Snark of—"

"LALALALA—I didn't hear you say that."

"Fine! Fine, I'm no one."

"Just as the prophecy foretold . . ."

Jaqof grabbed Malarya's dangly eyes and shoved them back into their sockets, restoring her sight. He dropped a slip of paper into her collection box, kicked it over, and walked away. Written on the paper was Malarya's first official assassination target: a traveling actress in a local production of *Westopolis: The Musical!* Malarya excitedly grabbed her sword, Noodle, and ran to the theater.

Upon joining the audience, Malarya clutched Noodle and identified her target as the lead of the show. Malarya watched the actress nervously, unblinking, clutching her sword so hard her knuckles turned white, but as the show went on, she found herself taken by the mystic beauty of the theater. She laughed. She cried. By the end, she was singing along:

> "... *AND THAT'S WHY THEY CALL IT,*
> *THAT'S WHY THEY CALL IT,*
> *THAT'S WHY THEY CALL IT,*
> *THAT'S WHY THEY CALL IT,*

*THAT RIGHT THERE? THAT'S WHY
    THEY CALL IT,
OH YEAH, THEY CALL IT,
OH MAN, DO THEY CALL IT,
AW GOD, THEY CALL IT,
OH OH OH—OW, OW, SERIOUSLY
    OW. SERIOUSLY. STOP. THEY
    CALL IT,
OH MY GOODNESS…DO YOU SEE
    THAT? WHAT IN THE WORLD IS
    THAT
THING? IT'S…OH GODS, IS IT OOZ-
    ING? OH NO, OH NO, IT'S GIVING
BIRTH. THE CHILDREN! PROTECT
    THE CHILDREN! NOOOOO!
    GODS,
WHY?! WHY?! WHY HAVE YOU
    SENT THIS THING TO US?! WELL
    THAT
THING RIGHT THERE'S WHY THEY
    CALL IT,
THAT'S WHY THEY CALL IT,
THAT'S WHY THEY CALL IT
    WESTOOOOPOLIS!
THAT'S WHY THEY CALL IT."*

Malarya wept. That *was* why they called it Westopolis. The show was hard to follow, but something about it kept Malarya's attention: the nudity.

After the show, Malarya thought deeply about her target's performance—she decided not to kill her, moving Noodle off the actress's throat after cornering her backstage. The actress gasped for air. "Thank you," she said, through tears, "*That's* my *singing* throat!" They shared a laugh, and an arrow flew through the window and into the actress's eye.

Malarya ran—the Tasteless Men knew of her betrayal of orders, and they would stop at nothing to kill her. An assassin chased Malarya through the shady, disease-ridden alleyways she once called home. The assassin was gaining. Panicked, Malarya ran into the nearest open door and just prayed it was a no-assassins-allowed establishment.

Beyond the door was complete darkness; the two were sightless, but Malarya had picked one thing up during her training that the assassin had not: night-vision goggles.

Noodle plunged through the assassin's heart, quickly and painlessly. Then through the assassin's head, also quickly, less painlessly. Then just a full slice down the middle. Malarya stood above her would-be killer's body. "Well...I guess Noodle made...*al dente* in your skull." Malarya smirked, though her people were still millions of years away from inventing pasta.

There was nothing left in Blahblahblahvos for Malarya—yet she couldn't stop herself from returning to Jaqof Cigar for a final word, and maybe a few faces.

"Finally, a girl is no one," he said upon seeing her.

"Stop saying that." Malarya was having none of it today.

"A girl is no one. A girl is no one. A girl is no one."

"Stop it! I said stop!"

"No one no one no one!"

"A girl is Malarya Snark of Wintersmells, and I'm going to go kill Walty Fuck and all his fucking Fucks, and there's nothing you can do to stop me!" Malarya pocketed six or seven faces and left—just as Jaqof thought of the perfect comeback.

❦

Malarya stood at the entrance of the ancestral castle of House Fuck. She clenched her fists and repeated her kill list: "Cervix Bangsister. Walty Fuck. Ed...Ed something. Uh...Deaddard Snark. No." A servant woman approached her, and she froze.

"Welcome!" the woman said giddily. *Thank the Gods*, Malarya thought. *They speak British here too.* Malarya killed the woman.

"Well, it looks like *Noodle* was 'welcome' in your skull—no, wait, well, it looks like—looks like the ides of March was in your head all along—wait, no I got it, guess that's why *they* call *it* the *blues*—wait—" There was no time. Malarya donned the servant woman's attire, then set to cutting off the woman's face. After several dozen attempts and false starts, Malarya messed it up really badly several more times. When she finally succeeded, the face was in tatters, bleeding all over the place, most of it still on the woman's corpse. Malarya was pretty sure she was doing something incorrectly, but she shrugged, stapled the mangled face to her own, and rushed inside.

She entered Walty Fuck's chambers at suppertime. Walty was by far the oldest man Malarya had ever served dinner to while in a disguise.

"Servant girl! Servant girl!" Walty was wearing triple-bagged adult diapers.

"Good eve, my lord," Malarya said politely.

"You know, you've got a real tight...something. I don't know, tell everyone I said something sexist. And what's going on with your face? It almost distracted me from only staring at your tits this whole time."

"I've prepared your supper, my lord."

"You know, let's do things differently tonight. Fetch me my sons. Not including the fat one. Wait, wait, wait—yes, including the fat one."

Malarya smirked. "I already have, my lord." She produced Walty's supper—his sons' bodies, barely cooked, on skewers.

Walty sat in shock. He yelled, "Get. Out. Of. My. Head." He began to devour his meal, which he referred to as "son kebab."

"My—my lord, these are your *actual* sons."

"I know, right?" He spoke with a mouthful of cheekbone. "It's like, I think it, you do it. Incredible work, servant girl."

Malarya grew frustrated and removed the servant girl's face from her own. "Well, well, well!" she proclaimed. "The time has come!"

"Oh my Gods. I. Love. Son kebab. Do we have more sons?" Walty wasn't paying attention.

"Hello! It's me! Look! Weren't expecting that, were you?"

Walty thought for a moment. "Who?"

"Me! Come on, it's me, Malarya! Pretty surprising, huh?"

Walty thought for a second, then continued eating.

"You killed my whole family? At a *wedding*?"

"This is preposterous, girl," Walty said, spitting out a chunk of foreskin.

"I'm a Snark, and I'm here to kill you, okay?"

"No, I get it, but how was I supposed to recognize you?"

"Because, you—because—no, yeah, you're right."

"You know, for a Snark you sure are a nice slice of—"

Malarya slit Walty's throat. He spoke his final words: "Wait . . . were those my REAL SONS?" He died, and Malarya laughed loudly—she was remembering "*that's* my *singing* throat!" from earlier.

"And *that's* why you don't have a destination wedding. No. Okay. And *that's* why you always bring a plus-one— that's why you—" No time.

That night, Malarya assembled the entirety of House Fuck while wearing Walty's face. She had never known the man in life and so would have to guess as to how he would have acted at one of these feasts. Malarya, as she assumed Walty would, stood to give a toast.

"You might be wondering why I gathered you. That's, well, you know, that's a very valid question. It's—you know, that's the thing about us, about House Fuck, you know, we're—we eat together, we eat together often, and uh—"

"Why is Walty Fuck's face stapled to yours?" a faint voice called out.

"Ahh, you know, and we're always busting each other's balls too, right? Like this guy over here." Malarya stumbled as she tried to point, dropping her wine. "But—but it's all in good fun, here! You know, here in House Fuck it's all in good fun. You know, I'm, you know, I'm Walty Fuck, I'm the real Walty Fuck, and, truly, I'd truly take a bullet for any of you. Except Uncle Charlie—where is that troublemaker?! Ahh, kidding, kidding, busting your balls, Uncle C, I'm just busting your balls, you know how we do that here."

"Are you a female child?" the voice beckoned.

"Yeah, well... that's, you know, we've got good wine, good food, the moon is out, there's... birds exist, and, essentially, you know, we stick together, but that doesn't mean we don't bust balls. We do. And, you know, fuck the Snarks, you know? I'm glad that we killed—" Malarya choked up—"that we killed—their whole family, I'm—I'm—it's good, I'm good, and, on a night like tonight, you know, where the moon's out, the balls are being busted, et cetera. You know, it makes me think—"

"Seriously, who are you?"

"I mean, I, me personally, I—Walty Fuck, that is—love my family. Family is really a gift, like I said, and you know, the moon's out tonight, it's a great night, yada yada, and…ahhhh, screw it! Let's feast!" Malarya ripped up her fourteen remaining note cards.

The tables were lined with chalices. What the Fucks didn't know was that Malarya had spiked their wine with three hundred cold hard cc's of Westopolis's most ambiguously labeled over-the-counter laxatives; what Malarya didn't know was that the Fucks had collectively not defecated in seven years. The Fucks gulped down their wine, and almost immediately the floor started rumbling. Within seconds a raging shitstorm erupted out of the entire Fuck family. There was shit in every chalice. There was shit between every floorboard. Falling from the ceiling, shit. There was shit outside, looking in through the window because the building was at shit capacity. There was even shit just hanging out, not in any one place in particular.

Malarya swam to each Fuck, killing everyone responsible for the death of her family and also killing the ones who were innocent but begging to be killed because of the shit. The crazy thing was, their bodies, even after all the shitting, emptied their bowels again upon death.

After some time, Malarya was sure that every Fuck was dead. She went back and stabbed them all, to be sure, and then she set the castle on fire and stepped outside. She then stepped back inside and stabbed them all several more times than before—hundreds of times, really—and then really took her time walking back outside. As she watched the blaze, she tore off Walty's face, and, with it, a significant amount of her own.

Malarya had finally avenged her family's death and could cross Walty's name off of her kill list. But she couldn't help but feel that she was forgetting something. "Cervix Bangsister. Deaddard Snark. Ed . . . Goddammit, Ed . . ." *Surely that isn't right?* thought Malarya.

And there he was. As if the Gods had placed him before her, Malarya looked upon the one and only Edward Christopher Sheeran, singer of hits such as "Shape of You" (2017) and "I See Fire" (2013, *The Hobbit: The Desolation of Smaug* soundtrack).

"Sorry to bother!" he said, approaching Malarya. "I'm looking for Walty Fuck?"

"You are?" Malarya asked, feeling a twitch in her sword arm.

"Yeah, an old friend!" Things were looking pretty grim for Ed.

"An old . . . friend?" Malarya stepped closer, the twitch in her arm now a violent stabbing motion.

"Yeah, an old friend! A pal! I played at his daughter's wedding!"

"You . . . did, did you?" Malarya unsheathed Noodle.

"Right, yeah! Come on, you remember, it was cold out, he killed a whole bunch of people right as I launched into 'Photograph' (2015), hilarious! Old pal. Where's he about then?"

Malarya brought her sword down upon Ed, slicing him in half. There was no time for a catchphrase. She pulled out a cloth and cleaned off Noodle before Ed's two half corpses hit the ground. A nearby horse approached Malarya to see what all the commotion was. The horse looked at Ed's corpse and then at Malarya, and as they locked eyes, it gave her a knowing glance that all but screamed "NYEYEYEYEEHEHEHHHHHHH." Malarya mounted the horse, pointed it north, and set it in motion. She had to get to Wintersmells. She had to find her family.

As the horse walked on, Malarya pulled out her list to update the names after the day's work. She read the list silently, then looked back at Ed and let out a chuckle as his two cross sections shrank to a speck in the distance. She had been right. He wasn't on the list after all.

Jon

Jon rode to Wintersmells on horseback with Pantsa, Ser Boats, Whoremund, a handful of Lords, a handful of Ladies, a whole lot of ladies, and a several-thousand-person army comprised of both Mildlings and Snark soldiers.

Once they arrived Jon explained that he would negotiate with Handsy Boytoy before their battle, but also just catch up with him. Handsy had abused Jon's sister Pantsa, tortured his best friend Peeon, and usurped the title of Lord of Wintersmells and Warden of the North through deception and murder. *But other than that, Handsy seems like a pretty okay guy*, Jon thought.

"You really don't have to be here," Jon whispered to Pantsa when he recalled what Handsy had done to her.

"Wait, really?" Pantsa squealed and departed immediately.

Finally, after traveling on horseback for almost an hour, they only had twenty minutes more of horse riding to go before reaching Handsy. And then twenty minutes later, they realized they had made a wrong turn. It took twenty-five more minutes before Jon meekly began to approach Handsy.

"Surrender before me, bastard, and I will spare Rickety," Handsy demanded.

"Who?" Jon asked.

"Rickety Snark. Your brother? The youngest born of Deaddard 'Iron Neck' Snark?"

"You mean Bland?"

"No, not Bland. The kid said his name was Rickety," Handsy asserted.

"Rickety... Rickety... Not ringing a bell. Do I really have a brother named Rickety?" Jon asked.

"He's just fiddling with you, Jon," Ser Boats whispered into Jon's ear. "You most certainly do not have a brother named Rickety."

"He does! His name is Rickety, and he is eleven years old!" Handsy said.

"This is what Handsy does. He plays games with people," Ser Boats explained. "You mustn't let him get to you."

"Well now hold on, hold on," said Jon. "Has this, erm, Rickety boy, ever done anything of note? Anything at all that I might remember him by?"

"Well, no, I suppose he has not, but he is certainly your br—" Handsy was cut off by Ser Boats whispering to Jon again.

"You can see him crumbling. We've beaten him at his own game, my boy. We've beaten him!" Ser Boats and Jon high-fived giddily.

"Enough of the games, Handsy," Jon asserted. "We don't need to risk the lives of our men. Just our own. We can just settle this the traditional way: two guys, two knives. A fish-cutting contest. Winner takes control of Wintersmells."

"Jon Dough, why would I risk competing with you, the most legendary fish cutter in modern times, in a fish-cutting contest, when I know my army will defeat yours in battle?" Handsy asked.

"Because fish cutting is very fun."

"This is true. Well, I guess we have a deal—" Handsy said but was interrupted by one of his advisors, who whispered into his ear. "But I like fish cutting! It's a northerner's favorite way to pass the time in this godsdamn tundra," whined Handsy at the advisor. The advisor nodded calmly and continued whispering in his ear. "Fine! Fine!" shouted Handsy, unhappily crossing his arms and facing Jon again. "After much consideration I have come to the decision that it would in fact be prudent of me to decline your offer. I will see you on the battlefield tomorrow morning."

"We were actually planning a sneak attack in the middle of the night," Jon said. "I cannot tell a lie so I had to come clean about that."

"Come on, Jon!" Ser Boats seethed.

"Sorry, Boats," said Jon. "But I'm an honorable man."

"Then why did you make us spend hours planning a sneak attack?" complained Boats.

"Boats, I don't want to hear another word," replied Jon sternly. "Honor is too important. Well, I guess we won't do that sneak attack anymore. No more sneak attack, folks!"

"Ah man!" cried the Mildlings, jacked up and ready for a sneak attack.

"We'll see you tomorrow morning then," Handsy said, a devilish smile on his face. "Rickety will be joining us too. And my flesh-eating hounds are very, very hungry. I've been starving them for six months." Handsy's advisor began whispering to him again. "What?!" More whispering. "When I said starve them for six months, I didn't mean give them literally *no* food. What in the seven hells is wrong with—never mind. Just get some new, *alive* hounds by tomorrow morning. See you in the morning, bastard!" Handsy departed.

❧

The next morning, Jon and Handsy waited for each other to make the first move for what felt like two hours but was actually two hours and ten minutes.

"So do I just...tell everyone to charge or something?" Jon asked.

"I think so?" responded Ser Boats. "I've never really done this before."

But before Jon could decide what to do, Handsy, from the other side of the field, released Rickety Snark, who ran across the field toward Jon's men.

"This is too easy," said Jon happily. "They're just gonna let me kill this little kid."

"No, Jon, that's your brother Richard—" cried a Snark soldier.

"AHHHH!" Jon bellowed and charged toward the boy on horseback.

Handsy, meanwhile, aimed his bow and arrow at the young child. The first arrow missed him by two feet, and the second missed by just six inches. But then Boytoy shot his third and last arrow, which whizzed high up in the air and then arced and fell, landing directly in a patch of grass sixty yards to the left of Rickety. Jon arrived moments later, followed by his men, and slashed Rickety with his sword.

"Jon, it's me, Ricket—" *Slash*.

"Jon, I'm your broth—" *Slash*.

"Jon, please stop—" *Woosh*. Jon missed.

"That's your brother Ronald!" came a voice from one of his men.

"Wait, what?" Jon asked.

"It's me, your brother! Rickety!"

"Ah shoot, wait, give me a minute." Jon stood with his forehead in his palm. "I'm sorry, I just can't think of a Rickety. Unless? Wait? Do I have a brother named Rickerd? Maybe? Rickerd?"

"Yes, sure, fine, that's me!" Rickety gave up. "And I'm desperately injured!"

"Oh brother, I am so sorry," he said to Rickety.

"It's okay, Jon. I won't die if I receive proper medical attention."

"My goodness, I will miss the boy so much when he is dead," Jon lamented to the tears of those surrounding him.

"He was a good soul. He will indeed be so dearly missed," Ser Boats whimpered.

"Everyone, I'll be okay. I'm losing some blood, but if I receive medical attention soon, I'll be okay! Or actually, Smellisandre, can't you use the Fire Man's help to revive people?" Rickety pleaded.

"Oh, um, sometimes. But I don't know if I really want to bother Him with another favor, you know?" Smellisandre said, looking at her nails.

"You know what? I think I'll actually be okay," Rickety said, starting to stand up. "These wounds are mostly superficial—"

"I have to put the poor boy out of his misery," Jon said with tears in his eyes.

"Wait, no, no, no—" *Slash.* Jon slit Rickety's throat, as his men nodded in solemn approval. "Now let's win this battle—for my late brother, Reuben! He was as good a man as any. CHARGE!"

Jon and his men charged toward Handsy's cavalry. *Oh, whoa*, thought Jon. *I guess shouting "charge" really works.* Ser Boats led a flank that held back, because they hadn't all tied their shoes yet. Handsy remained on his side of the battlefield with his archers, commanding them to shoot whenever he got bored or aroused.

Whoremund found Handsy's second in command, Smalljon Bumbler, and each performed the standard pre-one-on-one battle routine of asking how each other's family was doing. Then, after requesting that the other send his mother his best, they began the rough stuff, insulting each other's mothers with the vilest jokes possible. Once they were both sufficiently offended, it was fighting time. Whoremund bit Bumbler's ear.

"Oh, sorry, I meant to bite your neck," Whoremund said.

"Oh no, don't worry. You can try again," Bumbler said and waited patiently, while Whoremund cocked his head backward and lunged for his neck.

"AHHHH!" Bumbler writhed in pain. "You piece of shit! That's my other ear!"

Meanwhile, other Snark soldiers weren't faring so well. Half of Jon's soldiers had already been shot by arrows, and the other half had accidentally shot way too many of those arrows at their own men.

There was a mountain of dead soldiers piling up in the northeast corner of the battlefield. It looked sort of like an inactive volcano, if an inactive volcano had a mountain of dead men on it. At the foot of the mountain, dozens of Snark men were badly injured and on the brink of death, when all of a sudden, almost as if by a literary device known as deus ex machina, a group of horses stampeded over them, killing most.

Finally, the men in Ser Boats's flank had tied their shoes, and they moved into the center of the battlefield, except for a handful who tripped over their shoddily tied laces.

Then, the rest of Handsy's foot soldiers arrived, surrounding the Snark men in a circle and pointing spears toward the center.

"What a phenomenal strategic move," Jon remarked. "I think what we're going to do is try to break the line at this choke point and then attack horizontally from there."

"Um, okay. I don't know why you're telling me this, but thank you," one of Handsy's commanders said. Jon tried to break the line at a specific choke point and attack horizontally from there, but it didn't work.

The Boytoys moved in further, forcing the Snarks to make a human pyramid to avoid the spears. As the circle began closing in, Jon's men stacked themselves five men high, then ten men high, then twenty, cheering and shaking their battle pom-poms the whole time. Finally, there was only room for one man to stand in the middle, which meant the pyramid could go on no longer, and the inevitable had come. Someone would have to stand in the middle, carrying all four hundred remaining soldiers on his shoulders in what was no longer a human pyramid but actually more of a human ladder.

As Jon climbed to the top of the four-hundred-person human ladder, panic set in. He knew his men could only balance like this for so long before the Boytoys formed their own human ladder that was even taller. Defeat was imminent. But then, from his position atop the human ladder, about twenty-five hundred feet in the air, Jon saw something over the horizon: an army of men marching toward them wearing backward helmets and retro throwback armor, chugging ale, banging drums, and chanting, "Let's go, let's go, let's gooooooooo!" The Brodies of House Theta, a raucous group of young men led by the mischievous Littledingle, had come to Jon's rescue. It was the most beautiful thing Jon had ever seen.

"We're saved," he said, shedding a tear.

"Scatter!" shouted the Boytoy commanders as soon as they saw the Brodie army. The Boytoys began to desert the field, fleeing in all directions, terrified for their lives.

The men from Theta House rode onto the battlefield howling their house words, "Don't Be a Bitch," and knocked Handsy's army off their horses while also drunkenly falling off their own horses. They pelted glasses full of ale at the Boytoy men's heads with perfect accuracy. They shoved hot sauce down their throats until they barfed. They duct-taped them to the bottom of their own horses naked. Within minutes, Handsy's army was decimated.

"Thank goodness, we'll all be okay," a man now pretending to be on the Snark side said.

"Where are we blowing up tonight, lads?" the Theta House pledge master shouted.

"Where are we blowing up tonight, lads?" the Snark explosions expert said.

"..." a man whose vocal chords had been ripped out said excitedly.

With the help of Theta House, the battle was won, and Wintersmells would forevermore be both under the Snarks' control and, like, *super* chill too. Jon chased Handsy to the castle of Wintersmells, but Handsy closed the castle gate just as Jon arrived. The door was far too heavy for Jon to open by himself. But then he remembered he had Wub Wub, a burly giant with door-breaking strength, who was an expert lock picker.

Wub Wub got the door open in thirty seconds flat. Jon's men piled in, and Jon found Handsy in the corner inside the castle walls.

"I've reconsidered, Jon. I think a fish-cutting contest for control of Wintersmells sounds like a great idea," Handsy said. "You know, that might not be fair actually, since you did just win this battle honorably and fairly—"

Smack. Jon struck Handsy.

"Enough of the games, Handsy! This one's for Rickety!" *Smack*.

"And this one's for my brother who just died, Reginald!" *Smack*.

"And this one's 'cause I like punching!" *Smack*.

"And this one's for my friend Ser Jacob, who also really likes punching!" *Smack*.

Handsy lay on the ground, bloody, bruised, and beaten. A couple of Jon's footmen discarded the Boytoy House banner and hung up the Snark banner, while the Knights of Theta House hung up a banner with a picture of a smoking-hot naked lady on it. All was well in Wintersmells, except for the mountain of dead bodies outside. That took a pretty massive cleanup effort.

"Hello?" a weak voice could be heard coming from one of the many piles of dead bodies. "It's me, Rickety Snark! I'm still alive!" whispered Rickety Snark, who had miraculously survived.

"Check it out!" said one of the footmen. "This dead body is pretending to be a fake Snark."

"Eh? Throw it with the rest of them." And so Rickety got tossed in a pile of corpses, still alive as ever.

꘎

"Peeon, I give you permission to torture Handsy Boytoy now that he's our prisoner," said Jon.

"Oh goodness, I could never lay a finger on him," Peeon said.

"Peeon, I don't really have a dog in the fight, but don't you want to get your revenge? Handsy is an evil man. He did evil things to you."

"Okay, I'll do it, Jon. I'm so sorry. I will never disrespect you like that again, sir," Peeon said, cowering from Jon.

"You really don't have to—"

"No, I absolutely don't have to, you're right, sir," Peeon whimpered.

"But you can if you want to."

"Right, sir. I'll go torture him for you," Peeon said.

Peeon walked along the dirt path toward the chamber where Handsy was being held and stepped on a patch of grass.

"Oh Gods!" Peeon cried. "I killed it! I killed the grass!" Tears streamed down Peeon's face. "Please forgive me! Oh, I'm a monster! I'm just a monster!"

After drying his tears and being consoled by Jon, Peeon entered the chamber of Handsy Boytoy.

"If it isn't Ser Reekopolis III, MD," Handsy said.

"It is, sir," Peeon said. "Wonderful to see you again."

"Well, come on, Ser Reekopolis! Punish me!" Handsy begged, licking his lips. Peeon wound up and struck Handsy in the thigh with the might of a feathery tap.

"Oh Gods, I'm so sorry, Lord Boytoy," Peeon lamented. "I didn't mean to—"

"Ew. Peeon? What in the seven hells is going on here?" asked Pantsa, entering the room. "Were you beating him? Could you really not see that he was getting sexual pleasure from that? Stop crying and get over here."

"Yes, Lady Snark," said Peeon wiping his tears. "Sorry for being a worthless piece of manure."

"Peeon, don't say things like that about yourself," insisted Pantsa.

"You're right, Lady Pantsa. I'm so stupid for saying that. Stupid, that's what I am," said Peeon, crying into her shoulder.

"Oh, Peeon, I hope I didn't give you the impression that I wanted you to touch me. I find your tears very disgusting. Why don't you go cry somewhere else?"

"Aw goodness, I'm so bad at crying," wept Peeon on his way out.

Once she was alone, Pantsa began to enact her perfect revenge on her ex-husband.

"Let's find out how loyal your hounds really are when I release them from their cages into your cell," she said. Handsy just laughed.

"Oh, Pantsa. My dogs will never eat me. They are far too loyal," Handsy mused.

"Oh?" remarked Pantsa. "But you said it yourself, Handsy. You've been starving them for six months. They're terribly hungry."

"Well, all of those hounds died in a tragic... starving accident. But I am sure these new hounds are just as loyal to me, a man they have never met."

Pantsa flashed a wry smile. Handsy began to sweat nervously. Pantsa opened up the cages and got to safety. All twelve of the hounds immediately walked out of their cages, whimpered, and then fell over sideways, dying of starvation.

"What in the fuck?" Pantsa said, disappointed.

"Did I forget to mention that the dogs we bought were also starving, my dear?" Handsy cocked a smile again.

"This stuff always happens to me. I want to go back to the Strip, where they don't have piles of gross dog corpses." Pantsa began walking away from Handsy, leaving him chained up in his cell. "Jon!!!" she shouted. "I need you to cut off Handsy's head for me! My dog thing didn't work. Jon? I'm not going to cut off his head myself!"

❧

"I am a bastard. When my family had feasts, I had to sit down there while the rest of my family got to eat at this dining table," Jon said.

"You had that even bigger and more expensive dining table all to yourself?" Smellisandre asked.

"Yes. It was quite nice," Jon said. "I have no idea why they let me have the better one."

Suddenly, Ser Boats marched into the dining room and pegged a small trinket at Smellisandre's head.

"What is this?" Smellisandre asked, rubbing the spot on her forehead where the trinket hit.

"You know *damn well* what that is!" Ser Boats bellowed. "It belonged to Stankass Boaratheon's daughter— oh shoot, I think that's the wrong one," Ser Boats said, putting the first trinket back in his pocket and then launching a small wooden reindeer at Smellisandre's head.

"That's the Boaratheon girl's toy!" Ser Boats screamed. "And you let her watch someone get burned at the stake!"

"That's not true."

"Oh. Really?"

"Yeah, no. I burned *her* at the stake."

Ser Boats couldn't contain his anger.

"You *what*?" Ser Boats seethed. "You monster! She was supposed to teach me how to read! And she only got to teach me words that start with the letter *A*. You wench! I will never be able to read the *B* words or even the damn *W* words! It was my lifelong dream to read the word 'wall.' And now I'll never be able to! I can only read 'apple.' Fuck 'apple'!"

Boats was furious. He looked around for a book, a scroll, any form of the written word to destroy, but the only books in the room were the ones he'd put in the fireplace earlier for warmth. He had to get his rage out somehow, so he just started speaking random strings of words and punching at the air in front of his mouth as he said them. It was enough to calm him down for the moment.

"I can probably teach you to read. I mean, I do have magical powers," Smellisandre said.

"Oh, really? That would be great. Sorry for freaking out about that kid you killed. Jon, you wouldn't mind pardoning her, would you?" Ser Boats requested.

But Jon knew he had to banish Smellisandre from Wintersmells or else have her hanged. Sure, there were other options, like not banishing Smellisandre and not having her hanged, or some lesser punishment like community service. Jon, though, was too honorable a man to let this pass.

"Smellisandre, you are to leave Wintersmells at once or otherwise be hanged as a murderer. You are never to come back," Jon said sternly. "Unless you really want to, I guess. Then I'd probably let you come back."

Ser Boats wept, but he understood. The Brodies of Theta House wept too, as the ratio in the castle got a little worse. And Peeon wept because he accidentally brushed Smellisandre's shoulder on her way out.

"Please forgive me, madam," Peeon cried.

As Smellisandre walked into the distance, she took off her necklace, dropped it on the ground, and instantly aged upward of ten, almost fifteen years.

"You mean to tell me," uttered one of the Brodies, "that the hot babe who was here just now . . . was actually a MILF the whole time?"

"Why?!!!" cried another Brodie. "Why does this keep happening to us?!"

"Fuck you, Jon! Fuck you, man! Make her come back, bro," a Brodie begged through tears between hyperventilated breaths.

But Jon would not sully his honor. Not even for a MILF.

☙❧

The Mildlings, the Brodies of Theta House, and the houses of the North all gathered in the banquet hall of Wintersmells and started bickering.

"We're all just a bunch of clashing groups with too dissimilar of backgrounds and customs to ever get along," a voice in the crowd said. "We could never be unified by a common purpose or a common ruler!"

"Exactly! We all agree!" shouted everyone else in unison.

"My father used to say we find our true friends on the battlefield," Jon said, finally breaking his silence. "Which is why my best friends are this rotting corpse to my left and Ser Trenton Prottlebottom, the rotting corpse to my right. But anyway, I need all of you here for when the White Wieners come. I know we all have our differences. But we just have to realize that all of you are wrong and have dumb beliefs. I'm the only person here who has good beliefs." The room devolved into more bickering.

"Jon," Lord Manweewee, one of the most respected lords in the room, spoke. "I didn't fight alongside you on the battlefield at the Rootin' Tootin' Bastard Shootin'. And I will regret that until my dying day, at which point I'll probably feel pretty good about that decision."

"I never thought we'd find another true king in my lifetime," Lord Blubber, another senior lord, jumped in. "And we haven't. But Jon, you seem like a pretty decent guy, and if you want to be King in the North, I don't feel like it's really within my authority to stop you."

"Jon Dough is the fucking man!" the Head Brodie of Theta House shouted. "Let's get this guy domed the fuck up with a king's crown!"

"King! King! King! King!" the Brodies of Theta House shouted in reference to Blake King, a member of Theta House, who was chugging a keg of beer.

"And Jon, we think you should be King in the North!" the Head Brodie bellowed.

"King in the North! King in the North! King in the North!" the crowd chanted euphorically. This time, it was in reference to Jon Dough. Or maybe it was still in reference to Blake King. The man chugged a lot of beer.

Bland

It was the dead of night. Blandon Snark arrived at Wintersmells after a thousand-mile journey down from north of the Trench. He'd walked the whole way on his hands, doing a handstand pushup every few steps. *I've hardly even broken a sweat*, he thought. *In terms of upper body strength*—Bland took a moment to call upon his Pink-Eyed Raven abilities and survey the entire world—*I am the 238th strongest person in the world*. He was right.

After vaulting himself over the gates, Bland made his way to the bedroom of Hamwell Tardy, the only man still awake in Wintersmells. Ham had himself only just returned to Wintersmells from Citadel State University, where he read books all day so that, one day, he might become a maester who was simply allowed to read books all day.

Thud-thud-thud. Bland knocked on the door with one hand while doing tricep dips on the other. A friendly round face opened the door. "Hamwell Tardy," said Bland.

"How'd you know my name?" asked Ham. "Are you some sort of magical person with all-seeing and all-knowing powers? Some sort of raven-like being with some sort of conjunctivitis colloquially called 'pinkeye'?"

"I'm Bland Snark. We've met multiple times."

Ham now remembered the boy and took him into his chambers. He gave Bland a seat by the fire and brewed a pot of tea. "Bland, you seem...different."

"That's because I'm the Pink-Eyed Raven now," said Bland (the Pink-Eyed Raven) (now).

"Oh...Well, I don't know what that means. You've given me no context, and you've stated that you're the Pink-Eyed Raven extremely confidently, as if that's something I'm supposed to understand immediately. Are you just going around telling people you're the Pink-Eyed Raven and expecting them to understand that?"

"It means I can see things that happened in the past," said Bland. "And I can see things happening now, all over the world."

Ham shot a skeptical look at Bland.

"For example," said Bland, "before I came in here, you were trying to eat a book."

"Shhhhh!" said Ham. "My lady friend Chilly is asleep in the other room. She *can't* know about that." Chilly had just had sex with Ham for the first time the other night, after he'd promised to stop eating books for good.

"I've come to tell you about a vision I've had," said Bland. "It's about Jon. No one knows but me. You see, Jon isn't really my father's son. He's the son of Yomomma Snark, my aunt. I watched her give birth to him. Now I've just got to find out who the father is."

"My Gods," said Ham. "When I was at Citadel State, I very conveniently came across an old septon's papers. There were thousands and thousands of septons' diaries, but luckily I only ever looked at this specific one. What an incredible, plot-advancing coincidence. This septon, well, he said he annulled RayRay Grandslam's marriage to Elitist Martell and held a secret marriage ceremony for RayRay and Yomomma Snark. If that's true, and if they are Jon's parents, then that means that Jon isn't a bastard at all. Can you use your visions to see if RayRay and Yomomma ever conceived a child?"

Bland's eyes shot backward into his head and crusted over with a pinkish-red color. He was wanking back into the history of the world. "I've got something," Bland said. It was Yomomma Snark and RayRay Grandslam, in bed together, approximately nine months before Jon was born. "It's promising, but to be honest, Ham, I've never had sex before, so I'm not sure if this is it."

"Don't worry, Bland, I know all about sex now," said Ham with a proud grin. "Describe it to me, and I'll tell you everything, champ."

"Well, they're in bed together," said Bland.

"Naturally."

"RayRay is lying down on his back."

"Oh ... okay," said Ham nervously.

"And my aunt Yomomma is sitting on top of him."

"Huh?"

"And now she's bouncing up and down on him, facing away from him."

Ham spit out his tea. "She what?"

"So is this sex? RayRay Grandslam...is he Jon's father?"

"I..." Ham's voice cracked. "No?"

"Do you not know?" asked Bland.

"We can figure this out. We've got this. I've got this," said Ham, drying his palms on his shirt. "So where's his, you know, where's his penis during all of this?" asked Ham.

"Inside her privates?"

"See, that's sex. That's sex right there," said Ham, feigning confidence. "And she's?"

"She's on top of him."

Ham slammed his fist down on the table in frustration. "Then—then that's just not sex!" Ham began to sweat profusely. "I'm so very confused."

"Wait, now they're changing positions," said Bland.

"Okay, good," said Ham, exhaling a sigh of relief. "I bet they're right about to start having sex."

"Wow!" said Bland with a grin from ear to ear.

"Is it sex?" asked Ham, smiling. "Is it, boy? It must be. I'm sure it is. If that's not the reaction of a boy who's just seen sex for the first time, I don't know what is."

"She's on all fours," said Bland, "and he's behind her. Sex...sex is incredible."

"I've got bad news," interjected Ham. "That's not sex, Bland. There is no way."

"But his privates are in her privates—"

"It's not sex!" shouted Ham. "It simply cannot be. I have had *it*, and frankly I've *had* it!"

"But Ham," he pleaded.

"No 'buts,' Bland!" Hamwell was upset. He stood up and began pacing around the room, wiping sweat from his forehead with a towel. "How in the seven hells could it come close to being sex if they're *not even facing each other*? Answer me this, Bland? Huh? How?"

"I . . . I don't know," admitted Bland. "I'm sorry."

"Now is this . . . is this monster," began Ham, "is he ever going to get on top?"

"Wait, he is! He's getting on top now."

"Thank the Gods," said Ham, relieved. "Sex . . . is imminent."

"Okay, she's lying down," said Bland.

"Sounds about right," nodded Ham.

"And he's on top."

"Here we go."

"And now he's moving down her body."

"I, I don't see why he'd be doing that considering—"

"He's kissing her privates," said Bland. "His head is completely in her privates."

"Gods dammit!" yelled Ham. "Is that even something? That's not sex, so what in the seven hells is it? Could that even possibly feel good? What are they trying to do here! What is that supposed to even be?" Ham's face had turned completely red. He sat down and drank a glass of water. "I feel dizzy."

Bland began to perk up. "Wait, Ham. Something's happening. He's still kissing her privates, but now he's completely rotated. He's kissing her privates, but she's kissing his privates at the same time!"

There was no response.

"Ham?"

Ham had fainted. Bland continued to watch his aunt and RayRay, but the two lovers soon finished up and went to sleep. *How do I find out if he's the father?* thought Bland. Then an idea struck him. Bland used visions to determine if Yomomma Snark had any other intimate encounters with men around that same time period. Unless yams and cucumbers of various sizes and shapes counted, she hadn't. RayRay Grandslam simply had to be Jon's father. *I knew it was sex*, thought a satisfied Bland.

"Ham, wake up," said Bland, lightly slapping the side of his face.

"Huh?" said Ham, regaining consciousness.

"Ham, I've solved it. RayRay Grandslam *is* Jon's father. And I had another vision of his birth. Jon Dough is not Jon Dough. He's Eggie Grandslam, the true heir to the Pointy Chair."

"My Gods," said Ham.

"Do *not* tell anyone," said Bland, making his way to the door, "Oh and Ham..." Bland stopped at the doorway. "It *was* sex." He exited and set out for his old bedroom.

"Chilly," whispered Ham. "CHHHHIIIIIIILLL-LLLLLLYYYYYYY!!!!!!!!!!"

Dennys

L and, Your Grace! Land approaches on the horizon!" cried the deckhand boy to Dennys, who stood stoically at the helm of the ship, watching her dragon children soar through the sky playing a game of "bite-onto-each-other's-tail-as-hard-as-possible-and-go-deadweight-plummeting-to-the-earth."

"For the last time, Piffley, that is the floor of the boat," Dennys sighed. "This ship has a floor made of wood. Wood looks sort of like land on the horizon, except, no Piffley. No it does not at all. You need to stop looking down at your feet when on the lookout for land on the horizon."

A drunken Beerion stumbled up to the boy and smacked him sternly on the shin. "Come now, Piffley. We don't want Her Grace to go mad on the journey to

Drunknstoned, do we? Be a good lad and sweep the top of my head. I'm afraid I fell asleep in the dustiest corner of this ship's brothel again last night."

"The ship does not have a brothel, my lord."

"Do not be an idiot, Piffley, of course the ship has a brothel. Down below. Immediately next to the galley."

"My lord, that is the room where the cook stores the dead walruses that wash aboard. Mm-mm-mm. Walrus on a stick. Walrus on a plate. Those cooks sure do know what they are doing with those piles of dead walruses that they keep in that room. That room that is not a brothel. Beerion?"

"Sweep. My. Head."

"Aye, my lord," Piffley said, still proud that he had just found land for the tenth time on this voyage already.

"Now, Your Grace," Beerion started cautiously, "the boy does provoke a question most intriguing."

"Oh does he?"

"It's just, well, we have been traveling for quite some time now. Are you sure we *are* approaching Drunkn-stoned? Our rations run scarcer each day. The Cloth-khaki grow impatient on these ships without ample space for their horses to roam and play horse-and-go-seek."

Dennys turned and looked down at Beerion. "Have you heard the story of the Dragon and the Dwarf?"

"Your Grace?"

"There was once a great queen. Let's call her Den-nyz, with a z. And *she* was, let's say, a dragon. Actually three dragons." As she spoke the sky began to darken, and the dragons stopped their game to begin circling the ship. "One day a dwarf, whose name was, hmmm, I don't know, what is a good name for a dwarf, hmm, *Beerion*, questioned the three dragons' sense of direction toward their home. A home where they rightfully belonged and had a perfect internal compass toward."

"This can't possibly be a story that already existed—"

"And the three dragons did not like having their sense of direction questioned! They did not like it so much that one day they *killed* everything in the entire world!" Draggin, Dragun, and Jragon lowered even closer to the ship.

"Your Grace," Beerion stammered, watching the sky, fear in his eyes. "I meant no disrespect. I am sure we will arrive in Drunknstoned in no time at all!"

"I, Dennys Grandslam, Mother of Dragons, Daughter of the Land of Drunknstoned, Rightful Heir to the Pointy Chair, Breaker of Chains, and Queen of the Seven Kingdoms, can hear the call of my home. I will tell you, dwarf, when we are near! And until that day, I suggest you keep your mouth shut."

The ship came to a screeching halt as it bottomed out on the sand. "We are here," said Dennys.

The castle of Drunknstoned protruded magnificently over the high mountains that guarded it from the coast. *Just as magnificent as I remember from years ago*, Dennys thought. *Yes, yes. Magnificent and beautiful.* She squinted her eyes to take a closer look. The castle had completely gone to shit, she realized.

During Stankass Boaratheon's tenure at Drunknstoned, the fortress was laid largely to waste. Whispers around the Seven Kingdoms said he had gone mad at some point after first sticking his penis inside Smellisandre and before first lighting a person on fire to allegedly gain a strategic advantage.

An obsession with burning people alive for even the smallest gain possessed Stankass. To ensure his breakfast did not contain any food-borne pathogens, a threat he did not understand at even the most basic scientific level, he would sacrifice fourteen of his most valiant men to the Fire Man. To be sure his pillow was properly fluffed before he laid his head down for rest, he would burn ten of his best pillow fluffers.

Time proved this practice to be an unsustainable way to govern a city. When he finally saw fit to move north and march his army toward Casablacka, he left behind sixty villagers to keep Drunknstoned under Boaratheon reign and then promptly shot flaming arrows into their quarters and asked the Fire Man in return to keep those men safe.

Thus, as Dennys and her cohorts made their way inside the walls of Drunknstoned, they were greeted only by the ashes and bones of sixty villagers. Sixty villagers, who will now be named: Christopher. Sixty of Stankass's best Christophers died that day he rode for Casablacka.

"My legs could use a rest and my tummy a cold ale," Beerion complained to Dennys. "Must you really walk through every single empty tower and stare off into the distance before saying, 'Shall we begin?' and then leaving? Leaving, I might add, just to do the same fucking thing in the next tower?"

Dennys pushed open a hearty oak door to reveal the room at the top of the tower they had been slowly ascending. She walked to the window and stared dramatically into the deep blue ocean. The jagged, dragon-toothed coastline cut into the waves like a stick of butter cutting through something much softer than butter. She turned around and looked to Beerion, Ms. Andei, and Dog Shit.

"Shall we begin?" she said absentmindedly and left the room to walk back down the stairs.

"Enough!" Beerion screamed. "Begin what?!"

Dog Shit tensed his sword arm, roused by the dwarf's moment of insolence. Stress was in the air. It was moments like this when he wished he had a butthole to clench.

"Your Grace," Beerion offered, lowering his head in apology for his outburst.

"You would be wise to trust in me at a time like this, dwarf."

"Your Majesty! Laaaaand!" cried Piffley the deckhand.

"Piffley, it is 'Your Grace,' and for the love of the Gods, you are looking through binoculars at the floor of one our ships. We are on the fucking land, Piffley," Dennys exclaimed.

Piffley looked contently to the west. *A job well done*, he thought. *Land found again*.

❧

"—because the Bangsister army has never been defeated in an open field, while trapped by steep mountains to the west and deep, cold water to the east," Lemme Bangsister bragged as he trotted along on his horse, Horse Slayer. Since becoming crippled, Lemme had felt quite emasculated by Horse Slayer. Every peasant in every corner of the Seven Kingdoms fancied himself a comedian when catching sight of Lemme's prosthetic. Was it his fault that he'd had his head cut off? Was it his fault that his father gave him a new head made of gold, the most conspicuous material? Was it his fault that the blacksmith who made the head had a slip of the hand while staring at a pretty lady and made the eyes crooked? Yes to all three. And on top of that, there was that damned horse. Always prancing and dancing along with his precious, still-intact head and his correct eyes. The feeling of emasculation grew so powerful that before setting out on their journey to Drunknstoned, Lemme decided to cut off his horse's butt and replace it with a hump of bronze. This caused Horse Slayer to trot with a very noticeable and debilitating limp. As such, the army had been considerably slowed down due to Lemme's insistence that he ride in front.

"Aye," LeBronn said like a fucking beast—*God, I love this character. George Martin here. Sorry.* "But that's surely because no Bangsister army has been stupid enough to find themselves in such a situation. You mean to get us all killed traveling like this."

"You and I both know the only threat to an army this size is these alleged Grandslam dragons we have heard so much about," Lemme said while jerking off to a corn-husk doll of Cervix he had fashioned for him by the premiere corn-husk sorcerer in King's Landing Strip.

"Come on, do you need to do that while we're traveling?" asked LeBronn, disgusted.

"What I do in the privacy of out in the open in front of anyone is nobody's business. Least of all you. Now, as I was saying, these dragons—if they *are* real—still pose no threat to our army now that we have developed...the weapon," Lemme said smugly, tucking his corn-husk doll back into his sock.

"If that weapon works, I'll give you my left testicle," spat LeBronn.

"And if that testicle works, I'll give you my kingdom."

"What in the seven hells is that supposed to mean?"

"You have had sex with more whores than my brother. I am only saying it's odd that no word of a 'Bastard LeBronn' has made it back to us from the brothels."

"You're saying I've got bad balls? I've got great sperm, Lemme! Swimmers down there!"

"Of course you do," Lemme smirked. "No need to get defensive."

"Defensive positions!" cried the First Guard. The Bangsister army halted. "My lord," he continued to Lemme, "there is a man up there. Two hundred paces, straight ahead."

"Calm, calm, sir, erm, First Guard, man..."

"My name is Ser Pennybottom."

"Of course it is."

"We went to Kingsguard School together."

"We surely did, Ser..."

"Pennybottom, my lord."

"Yes, and may I help you, Ser..."

"Pennybottom."

Lemme distractedly fumbled with his sock, trying to get ahold of the corn-husk doll with which he had some unfinished business to attend to.

"There is a man just ahead of us, my lord."

"There is a what—oh yes! The man ahead of us. A most keen eye, Ser Unnamed Knight. A most keen eye indeed. Why, I may be speaking prematurely, but we could use an eye like that in the Kingsguard. Of course we would need to send you to the school—"

Ser Pennybottom sighed. "Yes, my lord. Now about the man, shall we send a rider toward him?"

"Why, let me handle this one. Whether this encounter requires diplomacy or force, I am surely the best man for the job." LeBronn rolled his eyes as Lemme urged Horse Slayer forward.

"She loves me. She loves me nut. She loves me. She loves me nut," sang Piffley as he wandered around plucking flowers in the field. He kept his eyes glued to the ground, oblivious to the massive Bangsister army that was but a hundred yards away.

"You there, boy," said Lemme as Horse Slayer pulled up beside young Piffley. "What are you doing out here?"

"Well howdy, mister! My name's Piffley, and I've been sent to pick flowers for Queen Dennys."

Lemme froze and looked back toward his men, who had begun to unload and set up camp for the soon approaching night.

"Queen Dennys you say..." Lemme said with an ounce of worry in his voice. "She sent you to pick these flowers?"

"Well ooooowee, mister! She sure did!"

"You were with her recently?"

"Darnnnn tootin'! She's just over that ridge right behind us, going on about some army."

Lemme stared at Piffley. A bead of golden sweat dripped down Lemme's face.

"Her army, that is," Piffley continued, "of dragons and Clothkhaki blood riders. Oh boy! Look at that there flower! It's gray! Like a horse!"

"That's a rock, my boy," Lemme said, his mind racing at the thought of what lay over the ridge. "Carry on." Lemme turned about and quickly trotted back toward his army.

"Who's the lad?" asked LeBronn.

"Never mind that. Men! Spears and shields! Take arms immediately! Fall in line!" Lemme commanded.

"What's the meaning of this?" asked the First Guard. "He is just one boy. Surely you are overre—"

Suddenly a thousand thundering hooves crested the ridge directly ahead of the Bangsister army. The Clothkhaki horde stormed toward the unprepared Bangsister men.

"—acting...Men! Spears and shields! Now!"

Yip Yip Yip Yip Yip Yip Yip. The Clothkhaki war cry was almost as intimidating as it was incredibly irritating.

"Good Gods. They yip at us," Lemme wheezed.

The Bangsister army quickly fell into a tight rank of spearmen and shield bearers. The wall of warriors provided some level of optimism for Lemme. Perhaps they would stand a chance against the vicious yippers coming their way.

"Men! Only a few times have the armies I've led been defeated," cried Lemme. "And I don't intend for *today* to be the first day that continues to happen! What do we fight for?!"

"Money!" cried the thousand Bangsisters as they braced for the riders' impact.

Just then, from the clouds above came a deafening roar. Piercing through the sky was Dennys on the back of her dragon Draggin.

"LeBronn . . . The weapon. Now," said Lemme, watching the sky with awe.

LeBronn rushed away toward the covered wagon carrying their secret weapon—the only thing potentially separating them from certain defeat. Dennys homed in on the left flank of Bangsisters and with a single command, "*Gasolina!*", set one hundred men ablaze.

Plop. A single tear fell from the face of a Bangsister soldier and landed in a cute puddle as three thousand horses with Clothkhaki riders swinging scythes from their backs violently trampled over the Bangsister front line.

"Bro, *fuck* this," a soldier said disappointedly as Dennys circled back and lit him and his brothers in arms on fire.

In the fray, one soldier was valiant enough to lightly scrape the shin of a Clothkhaki before being impaled by seven other riders and then burned to ash by Draggin. It was a massacre.

"LeBronn! Get the damn weapon ready!" Lemme cried in desperation. As he spoke, a mean-looking Clothkhaki rider hopped from his horse and landed right next to him.

"Yip, yip, yippie, yip, aghhh."

Lemme drove his sword straight through the throat of the rider. "Not today, death," Lemme said, confusing his catchphrase with a different character's.

"My lord, we are fucked," said the First Guard.

"We are not *fucked* until my sister and I are fucking each other, which we do not do," said Lemme Bangsister. "Now pick up your sword and fight, you coward," he said, driving his sword through another Clothkhaki.

They were in fact fucked. Draggin had made quick work of nearly all the Bangsister forces. The handful that remained alive were either deserting to the mountains or running to LeBronn's call for help with the weapon.

"Right, then, give me a hand with this, won't you?" LeBronn said, struggling to remove the weapon from the wagon it rested in. "Three, two, one, pull!"

From a sheath inside the wagon, they drew the longest, most magnificent sword the Seven Kingdoms had ever seen. Fifty feet long and four feet wide, the sword made even the most average-sized sword look smaller than, but otherwise identical to, it.

Lemme smirked. "Let's see how you handle this one, Dragon Queen."

LeBronn and the soldiers helping him tiptoed toward Dennys, who was having Draggin unleash a monstrous jet of fire on an unarmed Bangsister medic. LeBronn looked into the eyes of all his fellow soldiers and gestured to attack. They heaved the point of the giant sword at Draggin and managed to stick him just below the shoulder blade.

Lemme thrust his fist into the air triumphantly. For a moment it appeared that Draggin was mortally wounded. However, Draggin was stronger than he looked. And he looked like the strongest thing in the entire universe. He shook the sword and leapt into the air. All of the soldiers dropped the weapon and scattered as Draggin hurled flames at it, incinerating it in an instant.

"Those fools. Why did they insist on making the sword out of wood?" Lemme shook his head.

Then Draggin turned his attention toward Lemme and, with a few powerful wing strokes, rocketed toward him.

"If I'm about to die, at least I die with you," Lemme said retrieving corn-husk Cervix from his sock. Ser Pennybottom swiveled around to see that Lemme was straight in Draggin's path. He sprinted toward Lemme and hurled himself forward, tackling Lemme toward the safety of the lake. Seeing Lemme and the First Guard tumbling toward the water shot a shiver down LeBronn's spine. His mind flashed to the infamous unofficial Bangsister House words: "A Bangsister does not like being wet." He instantly sprang into action and intercepted the two of them right before they hit the water's edge, tackling them both back toward land. Certain that Lemme would forgive him, given the circumstances, another soldier rushed to the conglomerate of three men and tackled them all back toward the lake, away from Draggin.

This pattern of back-and-forth tackling continued for the next thirty seconds until Draggin descended directly on top of them. A soldier feebly tried to push the dog pile of men to the safety of the water, but his feet just slid in the mud. He was the first to burn. It would be a dramatic understatement to say that the fire unfurling from Draggin's mouth onto the men was not even hot at all. After a full minute of flame throwing, Dennys called Draggin off, and they shot back into the sky toward Drunknstoned. The Clothkhaki followed their queen back toward their castle, yipping proudly at their unconditional victory.

Moments later, from under the pile of charred corpses, Lemme and LeBronn emerged. They stared at the faint outline of Draggin's wings cutting through the clouds.

"Aye then," LeBronn said, brushing himself off. "Back to King's Landing Strip?"

"Yes," Lemme stammered. "Yes, let's go."

A few hundred feet away, Piffley stood up. Despite being trampled by nearly five thousand horses, he emerged completely unscathed. He dusted off his hands and looked at his feet. There lay the bundle of flowers he had been collecting, now trampled and destroyed by horse hooves. He shrugged his shoulders, began to whistle a tune, and once again began skipping around, plucking flowers.

All was peaceful for dear Piffley.

Jon

Jon was shitting out of his window when Ham burst into his room. "Jon—I know how to defeat the White Wieners!" panted Ham between bites of the turkeys he had in each hand.

"Yeah, yeah, I'll take three." Jon said what he assumed Ham wanted to hear, but his mind was just totally elsewhere.

"I stumbled upon a bunch of old maps at Citadel State when I was looking for porn, and I found this!" Ham finished his two turkeys and ate one more before holding up an old, greasy piece of parchment. Jon squinted at the parchment: it was extremely faded and stained with a white substance, but he could make out what appeared to be two islands shaped like breasts. He and Ham laughed and high-fived. Ham continued, "And later on I found an old map of Drunknstoned, which showed what seemed to be a huge deposit of gunnes hidden under the main castle."

Jon gave Ham an inquisitive look. "What in the seven hells are 'gunnes'?"

"You know, 'gunnes'? Like what I used to kill a White Wiener that one time? Remember? I killed one, and then everyone started calling me 'Trickshot,' and I had all those women throwing themselves at me but I couldn't do anything about it because I couldn't break my vows, and then they just kinda had sex with each other in front of me, and I tried to close my eyes but they held them open and made me watch? And then I held my breath so I'd pass out but every time I passed out they used smelling salts to get me to wake right back up and I had to watch them have sex? I told you it was the defining moment of my life and that I'd never be the same again? 'Gunnes'?"

Jon didn't remember the incident in question, but he couldn't bring himself to admit this to his friend. Especially not with that boyish grin on his face. "Nope, don't think that happened," he said after finally building up the courage.

Ham took out a piece of paper and started scribbling on it. "A 'gunne' is a weapon designed by the Thirsty Men—it shoots little pieces of metal that can pierce the White Wieners' icy hearts and destroy them." Ham scribbled for a few more seconds and then showed the drawing to Jon:

"See? They look really cool. And they're the only way we can hope to stand a chance against the White Wieners and their army."

Jon was intrigued. He pinched his stream of shit and got up from the window ledge, then wiped himself and grabbed his clothes. "Ham, if what you say is true," Jon held up a piece of paper, "then I shouldn't have just wiped myself with this invitation from Dennys Grandslam to come to Drunknstoned."

Ham had returned his full attention to nibbling on his turkeys. "Yes, yes. Sounds like a good idea."

"I have to accept her invitation and investigate this cache of gunnes. It may very well be a trap—but it's the only chance that my people have."

"Very well, enjoy your trip."

"No Ham—I have to do this alone." Without another word, Jon burst into a lengthy musical number and strutted down to the harbor.

❧

The spires of Drunknstoned rose up through the mist. "OH THANK THE GODS—LAND!" wheezed Jon. He stopped trying to drown himself and clutched tighter to the piece of driftwood he was floating on. He had refused the offers of the North's best sailors to accompany him on his voyage, as he didn't want to risk their lives if it turned out to be a suicide mission. Unable to steer, navigate, and operate the sails at the same time, he sank the North's most expensive boat a few seconds into the trip.

Jon needed to make himself presentable for Dennys and her court. He tore off his scraggly beard in chunks and wiped down his raggedy clothing with the bones of the few seagulls he'd managed to eat by luring them in with his testicles. He relaxed his eyelids to a normal level, as they had been fully open and dried out for weeks. He then sat up, adjusted his hair for a while, and passed out. His dreams were of the North.

When Jon woke up, he was at the end of a long table, facing a beautiful woman with silver hair. "Ah, you're finally awake," said the woman. "I am Dennys

Grandslam, Queen of the Sandals and the Thirsty Men, Rightful Heir to the Pointy Chair. And what is your name?"

"AAAHHHHHHHH WAAHAHWOHAHAH WHO?! WHOOOOOOOOOO?!" screamed Jon, his hair still impeccable.

Dennys's interest was piqued by this stranger. "Well, if the stories are true, then there could only be one man in Westopolis with hair as nice as yours. You must be Jon Dough, bastard of Iron Neck Snark."

Jon threw himself at the nearest chamber pot and ate its contents greedily. His mouth sufficiently moistened, he returned to his seat and said, "Indeed I am, Miss Grandslam, sir. The length of my hair is matched only by the length of my honor." He'd read that in a book once. Unsure of what to do next, he ran to the other side of the table and kissed Dennys's hand.

Dennys blushed, clumsily wiping off the excrement that Jon's lips left on her hand. "Ooh, I see you've read Grandmaester Pigfucker too? A scholar *and* a guy with long hair?" For a moment they locked eyes, each one caught in the other's gaze, the weight of their sexual tension matched only by the weight of their hands on their genitals as they were actively masturbating without blinking. Dennys suddenly remembered that she'd summoned Jon here for a reason other than pleasure. "Jon Dough, I invited you here today in order for you to swear fealty to me. As the last living Grandslam, I am the rightful heir to the throne, and—oggghhhhhhh"—Dennys took

a second to orgasm as she hadn't stopped masturbating—
"and I cannot allow for you to rule the North as its own
separate kingdom. Unless you want your people to face
the fury of my dragons, I advise you to bend the knee."

Jon didn't know what to say. If his father were here, he'd
probably do something cool with that iron neck of his, but
Jon's neck was nowhere near as uncuttable. *The North is
counting on me to lead them*, he thought. *There's no way
in the seven hells they would accept another leader, much less
one as foreign and young and female as this one. Think, Jon,
think...* Jon looked around the room, unsure of what to
do. He spotted a large bell hanging above Dennys's head.
*Oh! That's it! I'll throw my dagger at the chain suspending
that bell, and then it'll fall on Dennys and trap her, and
then I'll bang on it a few times from the outside and shout
something cheeky like "Really dinged ya on that one, huh,
Dennys?" and then while she's busy figuring out what in the
seven hells that means and recovering from the bell falling on
her head, I'll run down to the caves beneath the castle, grab
all the gunnes, and be on my way!*

Jon grinned, pleased with his plan. He looked back at
Dennys and saw that he was surrounded by several armed
guards, while several more were detaching the bell from
the ceiling and carefully lowering it. *Drat. Looks like I
was saying my thoughts out loud. Again.*

"You just said that out loud as well, Jon," pointed out
Dennys.

Drat. Looks like I was saying my thoughts out loud. Again.

Dennys looked at Jon while he stood there silently. "Well, Jon, if you won't pledge your fealty, then I will have to keep you here as a prisoner. But first—oghhhhhhh-hhhhhhhhhhhh"—Dennys orgasmed again, harder this time—"but first, what in the world are 'gunnes'?"

꧁꧂

Jon finished explaining gunnes, zombos, and White Wieners to Dennys. Even though Dennys didn't fully understand or believe what Jon was saying, she had to admit that Jon looked really cool in the drawing that Ham made of him.

"So, you see, Dennys, it's imperative that I get these gunnes back to the North if we are to defend the realm. If we don't stop the White Wieners, I'm afraid all of Westopolis will be..." Jon forgot what word he was going to say, but Dennys knew it was a bad one and got spooked anyway. "There's no point in you, me, or Cervix fighting each other right now. We're just wasting resources on a war that's small potatoes compared to Great Zomborian War I: The Reckoning." Jon had come up with that term himself. "I have a plan to establish a temporary peace. I'm going to lead a team beyond the Trench so that we can capture a zombo and present it to Cervix. Once she sees that the undead threat is real, she'll have to at least momentarily stop the foolish war over this continent— a continent that will soon be..." Damn, what was that word! "Anyway, that's why I came here to Drunknstoned.

113

Under this castle is a huge cache of gunnes that we need in order to fight the White Wieners."

"Jon, I must admit that I think you made all of that up on the spot so that I wouldn't imprison you. But if all it's going to take for Cervix to make peace long enough for me to build up my army and invade her city is for you to take the gunnes from here, then go ahead. They're taking up all the space for my man cave anyway."

As Dennys was turning to lead Jon down to the caves, Yora Mormon burst into the chamber. "Queen Dennys, my sweet!" he yelled. "Take a look at this—I just got it done today!" Yora ripped open his shirt, causing his colostomy bag to explode all over the Queensguard. On his chest was an enormous tattoo of an ugly doglike creature with the word "dennis" scribbled above it. "It's you! See? And look, I can make it talk!" Yora pushed together the fat on either side of his abdomen and made the dog contort in a weird way while he said, "Oh, hello, Yora, aren't you a handsome young man, hmmmm?" in a raspy, high-pitched voice.

Dennys had an idea. "Yora! Your tattoo, it's, uh, it's uhhh—I hate dogs! I love it! Wow, it's just great. Meet my friend Jon Dough—he's here allllllll the way from the North, and now he's gonna go back and bring back an undead soldier so that Cervix Bangsister will leave us alone for a while. How'd you like to go on a *special* mission for me and join Jon on his quest?"

Yora got so excited, his teeth went flying across the room. "Queen Dennyth, you can be thertain that I

114

exitht to therve!" Yora popped his dentures back in and continued, "So, Jon Dough, you fancy yourself a young adventurer, eh? Well, I'm quite the strapping swordsman myself! Hyah!" Yora struggled for a few seconds to unsheathe his sword and then pulled it halfway out and sliced his catheter. While his fluids leaked on the floor, he produced a huge mug of beer and proclaimed, "Or perhaps you think you can outdrink me? Why, I put all the squires to shame down by the stables! They don't call me 'Yora the Underage Drinker' just because of my nubile physique!" Yora put the mug to his lips, but his gout made his fingers scrunch up and spill the beer all over himself. He bent over to lap it off the floor and try to save face, but his back gave out on him with a loud *crack*, and as he collapsed he looked up to see that Dennys and Jon had already descended down into the caves.

Dennys led Jon by the hand down the stairs and through several small chambers. "I like to come down here when I'm drunk," said Dennys. "I blow out my torch and pretend that I'm a drunk blind person." Dennys took Jon deeper into the caves than she'd ever gone before; they found themselves in an enormous chamber. Before them was a tall pile of strange metallic objects. They shone brilliantly in the light of Dennys's torch and made the firelight dance around the cave walls. Right next to these metal things was a huge pile of gunnes.

"Wow, just like how Ham drew them!" exclaimed Jon. He ran up to the pile and picked up several gunnes, striking the same pose from Ham's drawing. As Jon posed, something on the cave wall caught his eye. He grabbed the torch from Dennys and held it up to the wall—revealing what seemed to be an old cave painting. It showed a man—the most ripped man Jon had ever seen—holding a bunch of gunnes in each hand and using them to shoot at a crowd of pale, humanoid figures. "This must have been drawn by the Thirsty Men," said Jon, awed by the vasculature and sheer girth of the biceps on the man in the drawing. He turned to Dennys so they could share the moment, but she was busy taking whiskey shots and shuffling around with her eyes closed, waving a white cane.

At that moment Yora's chair elevator reached the bottom of the stairs. He followed the torchlight until he found Jon and Dennys. *Alright Yora. You may be late to the party, but you can still show 'em you're capable of bringin' the heat*, he thought to himself. *Damn. I forgot my skateboard again.* He surveyed the room. *Eureka!* After quickly fashioning a rudimentary skateboard out of twigs and a DIY skateboard-building kit he found, he attempted a gnarly pop shove-it. He severed his leg without making the board move even an inch. "Evening, Your Grace," he whimpered from the ground.

Jon shook his head and grabbed the skateboard. He piled the gunnes on top and took trips wheeling them out to the beach, where one of Dennys's boats was waiting for him and Yora.

"Well, I guess this is good-bye for now," Jon shouted at Dennys, who was still stumbling around inside the cave. "Until next time, Queen Dennys!" Jon helped Yora load his walker onto the ship, and the two disembarked. As the boat set sail, Jon remembered the word he was trying to say to Dennys earlier. It was "thunderfucked."

⌇

The cold air up north by the Trench made Yora Mormon's arthritis flare up. That specific tingle in his joints meant only one thing. "It's about to snow," he said confidently.

"How can you tell?" asked Jon.

"No reason!" he shouted, darting his eyes around. "Uh, um, predicting weather is for those old-ass grand-pas at Citadel State. My joints are really healthy. We're just a couple of young stallions over here. Yeah, that's right, Jon and Yora: The Stallion Boys!"

"Um, okay," said Jon.

The two men approached the tall ancient gate to Yeastcrotch-by-the-Pee, the easternmost Night's Crotch castle built along the Trench—that ancient hole con-structed to keep out the zombos and the Mildlings. Leg-end had it that the Trench was so deep, if you fell in it, you'd never reach the bottom. It was hard to tell exactly where the Trench was, considering that the ancients had covered up the Trench with a magical thin layer of leaves to trick zombos into thinking it was solid ground. The Trench spanned the whole continent, from eastern coast to western coast, and had kept the Mildlings out for mil-lennia. It was quite an expensive public works project to keep up.

"The Night's Crotch men are going to freak out when they see me," Jon said to Yora proudly. "I'm sort of a celebrity in the Night's Crotch."

Jon opened the heavy gates to the castle in one swift motion. "Lads!" he shouted, sticking his arms out.

Jon was greeted with the sound of a cricket snoring. The hustling and bustling Night's Crotch men continued to go about their business, ignoring Jon and Yora.

"I said . . . LADS!" he tried again, this time sticking his arms even further out. Jon cleared his throat and stuck his arms out an uncomfortable amount. "Fellas! It's me, Jon Dough! Your old Bored Demander of the Night's Crotch!"

"You isn't Bored Demander," said one of the guards. "The Bored Demander is named Eddddd. Eddddd is the greatest."

Don't cry, thought Jon. *Do not cry.*

Yora tried to explain the situation. "No, see, he's, um, bros, with Eddddd. He's super, uh, tight? Yeah, tight's the word. He's really tight with Eddddd!"

"Well why didn't you say so?" said the guard. "Boys!" he shouted. "These guys are friends with Eddddd!"

The men all dropped what they were doing and raced to Jon and Yora.

"You mean you two met *the* Eddddd?!"

"You actually know Eddddd? Like *Eddddd* Eddddd?"

"What's Eddddd like in real life? Is he perfect? Is he glowing?"

Jon turned around so Yora wouldn't see him cry. But right before he could start spewing tears, he spotted some Mildlings. *Mildlings?* thought Jon. Surely they'd remember him!

"Mildlings!" shouted Jon. "It's me, Jon Dough, your savior!"

One of them looked up at Jon. "Oh yeah. I think I remember you."

"Remember?" shouted Jon. "You followed me to Wintersmells and risked your lives to help me retake my family's castle?"

"Oh, yeah," said the uninterested Mildling. "Jon Dough. Cool."

Everyone went back to work and left Jon and Yora to themselves. *Well, that's it,* thought Jon. *I'm a has-been.* Jon unsheathed his sword and began to contemplate committing suicide right there on the spot.

"Is that Jon Dough?" shouted Whoremund while eating a chicken drumstick, including the bone, in one bite. "Jon?" Whoremund dropped the rest of his chicken and sprinted for his old friend. "I missed you so much, Jon Dough!"

Jon put away his sword. *Thank the Gods,* he thought. *I really did not want to kill myself.* Jon gave Whoremund a big hug. "I told you these guys go nuts for me, Yora," he said, smiling confidently.

Whoremund hoisted Jon above his head, yelling about the greatness that was Jon Dough for his subordinates at Yeastcrotch.

Jon fluttered his long eyelashes and asked really nicely if Whoremund would help them capture a zombo. Whoremund agreed but said they'd need more men, and he had just the man in mind.

For weeks, Manwhore "The Clown" OfPain had been stuck in a Yeastcrotch jail cell. Every night he had night terrors about how scary fire was and woke up the whole castle screaming. Why was he afraid of fire? Aside from the normal reasons of it being hot and hurting to touch? You see, when Manwhore was a child, he tried to play with a toy that belonged to his older brother, Ser Greggy "The Building" OfPain. His brother got mad and pushed Manwhore's face into a fire, giving him a burn on his face that looked exactly like a dog. Because of this, people called him "The Clown" because of how absurdly clownish it was for a man to have a hound-shaped burn on his face.

"Fuck no, I won't help you," shouted the Clown, practicing cuss words to himself as Jon, Yora, and Whoremund arrived. In exchange for his helping them capture a zombo, Whoremund offered to free the Clown. "Fuck no, I won't help you," shouted the Clown. "Sorry, just a reflex." His practice had worked too well. "I'll come help."

The next day the four men set out for the lands north of the Trench.

☙❧

It was cold and dark north of the Trench. Unlike the warm boob I'm holding in my left hand and the hot toddy in my right. It's George—sorry, sorry, back to the book.

"Heeeeeerrrrre, zombo zombo! C'mere, zombo! Here, boy!"

It was no use. They'd been walking for almost a day and still they hadn't found a zombo.

"Mind if we take a rest?" whispered Yora, drenched in sweat and loudly wheezing, to Jon. "I think the Clown is past his prime, not young and spry like us. He needs a break."

"If only we could lay some sort of trap," said Jon looking around at the white, barren wasteland. "What do zombos love?"

"I couldn't help but overhear," said Whoremund, "but zombos love baby boys, and I happen to have this newborn in my rucksack."

"What? Why do you have that?" asked Jon.

"I don't know man. It's not a big deal. You can have it."

"We can't kill this baby," said Jon.

"I don't give a shit about the baby," said the Clown. "Let's kill it."

"Jon," said Yora, "I do give a shit about the baby, but I'm willing to sacrifice it to save humanity."

Jon thought about the moral implications of this for— ahhh, who am I kidding. Jon immediately took the baby and placed it on the ground. The four men hid behind a boulder while spying on their zombo trap. A couple hours later, they realized a zombo had been there literally since the moment they put the baby down and was still devouring the infant boy. The Clown sprinted out and got on all fours behind the zombo. "Tabletop!" shouted

Jon as he pushed the zombo over the platform the Clown had made with his back.

Whoremund picked up the zombo from the ground and grabbed its arms, shoving them repeatedly into the zombo's own face. "Why are you hitting yourself? Why are you hitting yourself?"

Jon took a shoelace and tied the zombo's feet together really tightly. The zombo tried to run away and immediately tripped and fell. The zombo got back up, and Jon shouted, "Your shoe's untied!" and then pushed the zombo's face up with his finger, even though the zombo did not look down at its "shoes" because it did not understand English.

Whoremund tied up the zombo's arms, legs, and mouth and then shoved it into a burlap sack. He swung the burlap sack above his head around and around and around, going, "Yeeehawww, I got a zombo!" until something caught his eye that made him stop. "Jon, buddy?"

Jon was too busy high-fiving the Clown and Yora to pay attention.

"Uhhhh, Jon?"

Jon was organizing a three-way chest bump with Yora and the Clown now.

"JON!"

Jon looked over and saw the horde of thousands of zombos standing in front of them, led by White Wieners on horses.

"Oh. Sorry about that Whoremund," said Jon. "RUU-UUUNNNNNN!!!!!!"

The four men took off as fast as they could, carrying the zombo with them, but they knew they'd never out-run the horde. *I've got it!* thought Jon, having one of his trademark "aha moments." *Zombos famously can't swim!* "Gentlemen, follow my lead," shouted Jon, sprint-ing off the side of the cliff they were running along. "Cannonbaaaaaaall!"

Jon made a huge splash in the lake below the cliff and began swimming to a small island in the middle. Next went in the Clown, who did a 360-degree cannonball, followed by Whoremund, who did a 540-degree cannon-ball *plus* a backflip, followed by Yora, who belly-flopped and threw up in the lake. As the horde of zombos sur-rounded the lake, unable to do anything that even resem-bled swimming due to the specific limits of their magical reanimation, Jon and the men knew they were safe, for now at least.

Hours passed, and the air became colder and colder. One bold zombo looked down and realized the water in the lake might not be so liquid after all. *Oh shit*, thought Jon. *Is this zombo going to run at us on the now solid ice, causing the rest of the zombos to realize they can do the same?* The zombo sprinted forward and immediately fell through the weak ice. *Phew.*

But then, several more hours later, another zombo tried the same thing, this time having several extra hours' worth of cold air on its side to freeze the ice even more solidly, and that zombo too fell through the ice immedi-ately. *Phew.*

For two weeks this continued. A zombo would get brave, sprint onto the ice, and immediately fall in. *Phew.* The men had nothing to eat except ice and the steady supply of fish provided by the lake. *Eventually the ice will get strong enough for them to reach us,* thought Jon. *Right? Or are zombos really fat? Will they never be able to stand on the ice because they're, like, super fat or something?* Jon chuckled to himself at the thought of the fat zombos. "Fatties," he said, making direct eye contact with the emaciated reanimated corpses around the lake.

At that moment, one of the zombos tested the ice for the first time in a couple days. The zombo carefully placed its first foot onto the ice. No cracks. The zombo took its other foot, moved it onto the ice, and began sprinting and immediately fell through the ice.

A loud "Fuck!" echoed through the valley. It was the Nighty Night King. He shrieked from atop the cliff where he was controlling the horde and started waving his arms around in what seemed to be a tantrum. The White Wieners next to him tried to calm him down, but it was no use. The Nighty Night King summoned all the zombos and sent them sprinting into the lake by the thousands. At first the zombos starting drowning, but soon enough their bodies piled up so high that other zombos could walk over them. Within minutes they'd reach the island and kill the humans.

"Men," said Whoremund, taking a big swig of ice, "I don't want to die a virgin. If one of you would do me the honor, I would be extremely grateful." But before Yora could enthusiastically agree, he was cut off by the sound of a dragon roaring. Dennys Grandslam had arrived with her three dragons to save the day. They all began to think victorious rescue music in their heads as they watched the dragons spit fire, burning every zombo in sight almost effortlessly. Jon and the rest rejoiced. Jon hugged Whoremund, and when the Clown refused to hug Yora, Yora hugged the zombo in the burlap sack.

Dennys did a few loop-de-loops on Jragon and then parked in front of Jon. "Miss me?" she said cockily.

"Actually yes, very much," said Jon, visibly showing signs of hypothermia. "What made you come save us?"

"I was worried when I hadn't heard back from you," she said. "Also I figured it would actually be extremely helpful if I brought the dragons. Do you realize how easy this mission would have been if I'd flown up here with you guys from the start? Did you see how easily I just toasted those zombos to a crisp?"

The Nighty Night King could hear her bragging from atop his cliff. He ripped off his tunic. Underneath he was wearing a track-and-field singlet and short shorts. He stuck out his hand, into which his righthand White Wiener placed a javelin. He counted out one hundred steps backward and then bounded forward. He sent the javelin soaring into the air with perfect technique. It stuck Draggin and ripped his stomach open completely. "Sixty meters!" shouted out one of the White Wieners holding up a tape measure underneath the dragon. The Nighty Night King began to high-five his friends.

Draggin's blood, internal organs, and stomach contents spilled out of his body onto Jon, Dennys, and the rest. "Eeeeewwwwwwwwwww!" shouted the men as Draggin's body went crashing down into the lake and sank to the bottom.

Jon, Yora, Whoremund, and the Clown hurried onto Jragon, hoisting the captured zombo with them. "*Skrrt skrrt!*" said Dennys in high Ovarian, wiping away her tears and snot. Off went the two dragons into the sky. Dennys wept the whole way home, making the men too uncomfortable to raise their arms and shout "Weeeee!" on what was their first-ever dragon ride.

Malarya

Wintersmells wasn't quite as Malarya had remembered it. The last time Malarya had been there, she'd been but a wee girl. So whereas the outer walls used to appear to be roughly seventeen times her own height, now they only appeared to be fifteen, maybe sixteen, times her own height. *Eerie*, she thought, approaching the gate.

Malarya spotted two men guarding the entrance to Wintersmells. One was tall and skinny, while the other was short and skinny. *Targets*, she thought, smiling. As she got closer, she noticed that they were donning House Snark armor. *Damn. Friendlies.*

"Trying to enter Wintersmells, eh?" asked the short one.

"Indeed. I'm Malarya Snark, daughter of Deaddard Snark, and I've returned home."

The guards looked confused. "But—but, Malarya Snark is supposed to be dead," said the tall guard.

If they think I'm an imposter, I'll definitely be allowed to use violence to get into Wintersmells, thought Malarya, hornily moving her hand over her blade.

"So this is fantastic news that you're alive!" he exclaimed.

Fuck! thought Malarya.

"What a miracle that you, Malarya Snark, have returned," said the other one.

Double fuck! thought Malarya.

"Now, we both trust that you are in fact Malarya Snark. However, technically we wouldn't be doing our jobs if we just let you through the gates without verifying your identity. Do you mind if we go get your sister Pantsa to come and verify that you are in fact Malarya?"

Close enough, thought Malarya. "What's that over there!" she yelled, pointing behind them.

"Huh?" said the guards in unison, stupidly turning around 180 degrees like idiots.

"I wish you hadn't made me do this," Malarya said unconvincingly before quickly pulling out Noodle and severing both of their heads. "Verify *that*," she quipped, sheathing her sword and chuckling to herself.

Malarya took a deep inhale and smelled the familiar stench of human poop being burned for warmth. *Home*, she thought, smiling. Now she was off to see Jon, the only family member she ever cared about.

As Malarya strolled along toward Jon's chambers, a distressed woman cried and ran toward the front gate.

"My sons!" she yelled. "My two boys were the guards of the gate! Someone's killed my two beautiful sons!" *Dumb old hag*, thought Malarya. *This place didn't used to have such loud and annoying people.*

Malarya tiptoed into Jon's creaky old room so she could surprise him by running up behind him with a sword. He'd turn around and draw his own sword, and they'd have one of their classic little practice fights. She saw him sitting down facing the fire. *I've got to maintain the element of surprise*, she thought, *or Jon will beat me just like he used to.* "AAAAHHHHHHHHH!" she yelled, sprinting at Jon from the other end of the room with her sword held high above her head. The figure in the chair remained still. "HIIIIIIIIIIYAAAAA!" shouted Malarya as she chopped her blade down at his right bicep. *SHWING.* Her sword bounced right off the bicep. It was far too strong to chop. She looked up at the man in the chair. It was not Jon Dough.

"Bland?" she said, disappointed to see her lamest brother.

"I'm not Bland anymore," he said, doing a pull-up on a bar he'd installed above the fireplace and letting his sense-deprived legs dangle into the burning fire. "I'm the Pink-Eyed Raven now."

"What?" said Malarya, confused. "What does that mean?"

"It's hard to explain," said Bland angstily.

"Can you try?" bargained a frustrated Malarya. "Like, can you try to explain a little? Do you expect me to know what that means just from saying it?"

Bland sighed as he switched from pull-ups to chin-ups.

"It means he has these visions called 'wanks,'" said Pantsa, entering the room. "That's how he introduces himself to everyone now, and he never gives any context or explanation. It's really not that hard to explain, Bland. You have to stop doing this."

"One hundred forty-five, one hundred forty-six, one hundred forty-seven," said Bland, unable to be distracted.

"Malarya, it's so good to have you back." Pantsa opened her arms and motioned for Malarya to come and hug her.

"That won't be necessary," said Malarya. "Is Jon around?"

"Jon's off to meet with Dennys Grandslam, the Dragon Queen. I'm the Lady of Wintersmells while he's gone."

"Oh," said Malarya. *Awkward*, she thought. "Here's the thing. Jon is sort of…my favorite? He's most of the reason I came to Wintersmells instead of going to the Strip to kill Cervix. You guys are great, and I think it's really awesome that you're here and we've reunited and all, but Jon is Jon. I mean, I love Jon like a family member. Does that make sense?"

"Jon should be back very soon," said Pantsa. "Until then, us three siblings can get reacquainted after all these years. What say we grab a drink and sing a round of 'Fair Wintersmells'?"

"No, yeah," said Malarya. "It's just I was hoping Jon would be here…now? Like, right now? Cards on the table, I just don't really know you two that well. Again, you seem great, but you're sort of just, like, casual acquaintances to me."

"Malarya," said Bland, having just finished his workout. *Oh great*, thought Malarya. *What does this one want?* "I have a gift for you."

"I have a gift for you," mocked Malarya in an idiot voice. "Fellas, you can't buy my affection with gifts. I'm just going to go wait outside until Jon shows up." She began to head out.

Pantsa coughed loudly. "Bland, is there a gift...for me?" She was visibly upset.

Before Malarya could reach the door, Bland uncovered the gift: a dagger made of Ovarian steel. "The gift is a weapon?" she said, clearly deriving some sort of sexual pleasure from the mere notion of violence. *Bland just moved waaay up in my favorite siblings rankings*, she thought. *New siblings ranking is as follows: 1. Jon; 2. The young one (What's his name? Rikert? Jernt? Jomb? Is he alive? Unimportant); 3. Myself; 4. Bland; 5. Snobb (rest in peace); 6. My direwolf; 7. My dead dad; 8. Pantsa.* "Where did you get a dagger like this, Bland?"

"Littledingle gave it to me," he replied.

"Littledingle?" asked Malarya. *What's a little candy-ass namby-pamby like him doing in Wintersmells?* she thought. *He uses lies, deceit, and trickery to kill people. He wouldn't be such a yellow-bellied pantywaist-milksop chicken-coward if he'd just use violence and weapons to do murders like I do.*

"I know Littledingle's facial hair is gross," said Pantsa. "And I know he's ugly too. And he's not very rich. And he tripled the amount of forced marriages I've been subjected to. And he kisses me in a weird way sometimes. And he talks about mother quite frequently in a way that is disturbing. But, at the end of the day, Littledingle lies a lot and is untrustworthy."

"So why is he here?" asked Malarya.

"Ah yes," remembered Pantsa. "Littledingle pledged the Theta House army to us. And I guess he also gives away sweet daggers now," she said, pointing to Bland.

"This dagger was intended to kill me," said Bland, "back when I was recently crippled, with my skinny arms...before I became *strong*." Bland kissed different muscle groups on his arms for fifteen seconds and then handed the dagger to his sister. "I want you to have it, Malarya. It might come in handy, you know, for stabbing."

"But Bland, doesn't that mean that Littledingle is the one who tried to have you killed all those years ago?" asked Malarya. "Could he be a force for evil who is out to get us? It would make sense, given all of his conniving and trickery, that this dagger is itself one more ploy—"

"Boooorrring!" interjected Pantsa. "You're overthinking this. It's a cool dagger. Hey, maybe you'll save all of our lives with it in a huge important battle or something," said Pantsa, sarcastically waving her hands and wiggling her fingers around. "I don't know. Just take it. It looks expensive."

Malarya shrugged and put the dagger on her belt. *SHING. DING. POP. ZAP.* Malarya heard the mouth-watering sound of swords clashing and went over to the window to see what kind of finger-licking violence was going on. It was Brian of Fart sparring with her squire, Godsdick. Brian was a far better fighter. Godsdick had fifteen local prostitutes behind him cheering him on with pom-poms.

"G-O-D-S-D-I-C-K! We all want to sleep with Godsdick to-day! (Hey!)"

Brian punched out all of Godsdick's teeth. Still the prostitutes kept cheering.

"Godsdick, Godsdick, he's our man! Fucking him after this fight is our plan!"

Godsdick was on the ground. As Brian got ready to kick him, he evacuated his bowels out of fear.

"'Hard to describe' is what we'll declare when you ask why Godsdick is so good with his penis in there!"

Behind the fight, a crying old woman rolled around in a bale of hay yelling hysterically. "DEAD! They're dead! Some monster has decapitated my boys!" *Shut the actual fuck up, old lady*, thought Malarya. *I'm trying to watch a fight.*

"Brian of Fart," said Pantsa, looking along with her sister. "She swore an oath to mother that she'd protect us, and now she won't leave me alone. Very annoying. Quite ugly, like you. Acts like a man, etc. You might actually like her, Malarya." Pantsa looked around, but her sister was gone. "Malarya?" When she looked out the window again, she saw her sister standing with Brian of Fart.

"Lady Malarya, perhaps you'd be better suited to spar with my squire," said Brian, pointing to Godsdick. But Godsdick was busy trying to break up a fight. The whores were once again arguing about who'd get to sleep with Godsdick that night, and things had turned violent. The ground was covered in torn wigs. Brian looked back to Malarya. "Well, I suppose I can spar with you while he's occupied."

Brian thrust her sword at Malarya, but the girl dodged it. "Pretty good," said Brian. She lunged her sword at the girl again, and again she stepped out of the way.

Malarya cocked her eyebrows as if to say, *I bet you thought this was going to be easy, huh?* Brian kicked her to the ground. She was twice as tall and three times as heavy as Malarya. Brian realized this and promptly began to pound the shit out of Malarya.

"That's quite a cute little sword you've got there," said Brian, laughing at Noodle. "But can you actually do anything with it?" Malarya spun around, escaping Brian's fists, and got to her feet. She grabbed a passing peasant carrying a pile of logs and slit his throat. "Touché," said Brian, impressed. Malarya sheathed her sword and shook her opponent's hand. "Who taught a girl like you to fight like that?"

Malarya chuckled to herself. "No one."

Brian of Fart stood silent and confused.

"Just a joke for myself," clarified Malarya. "It was these assassins called the Tasteless Men. They say that they strive to become 'no one,' so I thought it'd be funny to answer that way."

Brian of Fart stood silent and clearly bored.

❧

The next morning Littledingle awoke and went straight to the Wintersmells brothel. Waiting outside his room was Malarya, who'd been awake for three days so she could tail him in secret. Malarya didn't like that Littledingle was in Wintersmells, and not just because she was really racist against people from his region.

When he got to the brothel, Littledingle didn't solicit any sex but instead lectured the prostitutes on how to be better prostitutes. *This is odd, but I suppose it's kind of nice that he does this*, thought Malarya, spying on him from around the corner. *It's sort of a public service he's providing, I guess?* The whores kept offering to have sex with Littledingle, but he just kept yelling at them about how they needed to get on top more if they wanted to get repeat customers. *He's being pretty intense about this*, thought Malarya. Eventually, the prostitutes begged him to just have sex with them, even for free, if it meant he would stop lecturing about sex, but Littledingle would not budge. *Okay, this is getting pretty weird now*, thought Malarya as Littledingle screamed about the importance of foreplay until his face turned red. Uncomfortable watching any longer, Malarya left and instead decided to wait outside Littledingle's room to see what she could learn.

Two hours later, Littledingle returned to his room holding a stack of several books about the male G-spot. Outside his door the maester met him with a small scroll. "You're sure this is the only copy?" asked Littledingle. The maester nodded and handed it to him. "Fantastic," said Littledingle, looking around to see if anyone was watching. Malarya hid behind a wall just in time to escape his gaze. "I SURE HOPE NO ONE SEES THIS SECRET SCROLL!" he shouted. He walked into his room with the scroll, then shortly came back out empty-handed, locked the door, and left. *I've got to read Littledingle's secret message that he doesn't want me to see*, she thought.

Malarya studied the lock on Littledingle's door. *A bolted T-lock with three teeth per groove*, she thought. *I've dealt with these many a time before.* Malarya busted down the door with one swift kick. She began to snoop around and noticed a basket on Littledingle's desk labeled "Secret Scroll (Do Not Touch)." Malarya couldn't help but laugh. *What an amateur*, she thought. *Littledingle thought he could keep this scroll safe from me? Yeah, right. Certainly this is a message Littledingle does NOT want me to read.*

Malarya opened the rolled up parchment and read it.

Dear Father (Deaddard Snark),
    It's me: your daughter Pantsa Snark. You are a traitor, and no one is forcing me to write this. Admit

that King Jeffy is the real king. I also hate my sister Malarya because I'm a bitch. In the future, if Jon is ever bestowed the title of King in the North, I'm going to be jealous and secretly try to undermine his authority while he is away meeting with the Dragon Queen. These are all my original thoughts, and this scroll has not been doctored. I secretly think Littledingle is cute.

Love,
Pantsa Snark

It's a very good thing that I found this letter and wholeheartedly believe it, thought Malarya. She took the note and scrawled in her blood on the back, "Pantsa—I'm going to kill you and do treason because of this.—Malarya," and walked to Pantsa's room to leave it on her bed.

※

Pantsa sprinted to Malarya's room as soon as she read the note. She was furious. "Malarya! Your stinking note got blood on my bed! That is so gross and *not* okay!" she shouted, banging on the door. "Also the threats you made against my life and Wintersmells were bad as well," she said, deciding to enter the room. Malarya, however, was not there. How curious.

Pantsa looked around. She saw knives and swords and blades and knives, but what caught her attention was a bag sticking out from under the bed. She opened it up and found countless faces stacked on top of each other, all with labels attached to them: a messed up face labeled "Dad," an extremely fat boy's face labeled "Pie Bitch," dozens of faces labeled "Fuck Family Faces," a ginger face labeled "Internationally Renowned Singer-Songwriter Ed Sheeran," hundreds of faces labeled "Random Vagrant," a face that was just a label by itself that said "The Faceless Man," a face from a horse, a face from a bartender, and a face that was long.

"Gross," said Pantsa.

"Gross, indeed, m'lady," said Littledingle, suddenly appearing and pressing his lips to Pantsa's ear so she could hear his secret whispers. "Perhaps even, *too gross*." He quickly flicked his tongue into her ear.

"Oh. Hi, Littledingle," said Pantsa, wiping his saliva from her ear like usual. "What do you think is going on with Malarya?"

Littledingle began to massage her shoulders. "Sometimes, when I try to understand a person's motives, I play a little game. I come up with any reason possible to justify that they are guilty of a crime, no matter how far-fetched the reason is. Then I ask myself, 'Can I convince other people of this, despite how far-fetched it is?'"

"Doesn't that seem unfair?" asked Pantsa, applying a repulsive perfume that she carried around for when Littledingle was touching her.

"Perhaps," said Littledingle. "But if we use the logic on your sister, would she be innocent . . . or guilty?"

"I suppose guilty."

"Exactly. Now what do you say we go to my room and play pretend, eh? I'll be king of Westopolis and you'll be my queen."

"No, that's okay. You should do that without me."

As the two exited the room, Littledingle kept trying to convince her to play pretend with him. No matter how fun and educational he said it would be, Pantsa still refused and then lied about being late for a meeting and having to go.

"But I schedule all your meetings!" said Littledingle.

"You pretzel all my beefings? Sorry, can't hear you clearly, gotta go," said Pantsa, two feet away from Littledingle. She darted out to the courtyard. Littledingle hung his head and meandered around Wintersmells whistling tunes of sad country songs about heartache.

Phew, thought Malarya, dropping down to the floor. *I'm glad I leapt up and clung to the ceiling just as I heard Pantsa about to walk in, all the while holding an assortment of loose fruit. For a second there, I was sure I was going to drop a few kiwis onto Littledingle and give myself up, but luckily I stuck my foot out at the perfect moment to catch them. Man, oh man. And no way did I think I could balance that pineapple on the back of my head while it had three oranges resting on top of it. But I made it work. And when I started sweating and it all collected on the tip of my nose and it was about to drop onto Pantsa? I thought that was game over for sure, but then I was able to sort of snort it into my nose and not have them hear me because of that crow that squawked outside. Boy, oh boy, are my arms tired.*

⚜

The Wintersmells Great Hall was abuzz with hundreds of spectators. At the head table sat Pantsa and Bland looking somber. Two soldiers escorted Malarya into the room.

"We are gathered here today," began Pantsa, "to kill someone who is a threat to the North." Littledingle couldn't help but smile as he looked at Malarya Snark. His plan had worked. With one little forged note, he was able to turn the Snark girls against each other. Pantsa stood up and faced Malarya. "You stand accused of treason, murder, and attempted murder"—she abruptly shifted to face Littledingle—"Lord Balehead."

"Huh?" said Littledingle.

"Look at your face!" exclaimed Malarya. "Everyone look at his face. Look at how bad we got him. That face! You got GOT!" She began to do a mocking high-pitched squeak. "'Oooh, I'm Littledingle, and my plan worked and now they're going to kill Malarya.' IDIOT!" The room erupted in laughter. "Me and Pantsa met up and figured all this stuff out," said Malarya. "We just didn't include it in the book so there'd be a twist when we actually reveal that this is a trial for you."

"I, ummmm, I, uhhh." Littledingle's face was priceless. He really did look like a fucking idiot.

"You didn't just pit me and Malarya against each other. You betrayed our father, Deaddard Snark, and assisted in his killing," said Pantsa. "Do you deny it?"

"Of course I deny it!" shouted Littledingle, his voice cracking. "None of you were there, so I'm innocent."

Bland rolled his eyes back as they turned pink and crusted over. Suddenly he could see the past, and he *was* there. "You told him he was ol' 'Iron Neck' Snark," said Bland. The room fell silent.

Littledingle froze and clammed up like a frozen clam.

Bland continued. "You told our father that he was ol' 'Iron Neck' Snark and that there was nothing a sword could ever do to harm him."

"Pantsa," said Littledingle, "you must believe me."

"You knew he did not have an iron neck," said Bland. "But you still convinced him to go in front of the sword because you wanted him dead. You conspired with the Bangsisters to have him killed, and then you had him present his own neck for decapitation. And the whole time he thought his neck was too strong to be cut...all because of you."

"Pantsa, please," whispered Littledingle. "Forgive me."

Malarya approached him with a knife. "Don't worry, Littledingle. You're ol' 'Copper Throat,'" she joked. "This here dagger won't hurt you." Malarya cut his throat with a surprising level of difficulty. *Damn, he may really be ol' "Copper Throat,"* she thought.

Littledingle held his neck shut with his hands to try to stop the bleeding. "Pantsa, please. I'm sorry." *This fool won't die fast enough*, thought Malarya. She plunged her sword through his heart. *Try to keep talking after that.*

"Pantsa, forgive me," said Littledingle, standing right back up. "I really thought he *was* ol' 'Iron Neck,' okay? This is a huge misunderstanding."

You just don't know how to stay down, do you? thought Malarya. She cut a rope that dropped an anvil hung in the rafters right onto Littledingle's head. It squashed him straight into the floor. Crushed underneath the anvil lay his mangled body, his brain splattered on both sides.

"Pantsa, pleeeeease," said a muffled voice from underneath the anvil. "I think we can really work this out if we just have a mature conversation. Can I speak to you one-on-one about this? Again, I'm so very sorry."

So that's how it's going to be, eh? thought Malarya. *Good luck speaking with no mouth, head, throat, lungs, or voice box!* She cut each of the parts out of his body and diced them into bits with her sword. *My work is done here.*

Littledingle's hand shot up and began to make spastic signs. "It's sign language," said the maester from the crowd. "He says, 'Pantsa, I beg for your forgiveness. Stop. Let's just sit down like grown adults and work this out. Stop. I'm sorry. Stop. Please. Stop. I'm sorry. Stop. Sorry. Stop. Sincerely, Littledingle. Full Stop.'"

Malarya was furious. *Time to end this for good.* She doused what remained of Littledingle's body in oil and torched him. Littledingle went up in flames. In the air, his ashes arranged themselves to spell out "Pantsa, you've just got to forgive me. I love you. I'm sorry. Please. I really thought your dad *was* ol' 'Iron Neck'! I'm sorry. I love you. I also love your mom."

Malarya swatted at the ashes, scattering them around the Great Hall. When she was finished, Littledingle and his last words were gone. "Have a nice *die*, see you next *death*—wait, no, guess you love Pantsa and my mom *and* dying—wait, let's see you fuck my mom *now*—okay wait, wait, I got it: I want to watch you have sex with my mom." Satisfied, Malarya dusted off her hands and strutted out of the Great Hall, slamming the doors behind her, the ash she had thrown everywhere causing all the people trapped in the hall to cough, several of them to death.

Dennys

D o you want to do it again?" asked Dennys, splayed out on her bed and seductively rubbing her tummy.

"Again?" asked Jon. "But we've already done it so many times."

"Please. For me."

"You're insatiable."

"Just once more."

"Okay, but this is the last time." said Jon. "I, Jon Dough, do bend the knee and pledge the North to Queen Dennys Grandslam."

"Yes! Oh hell yes! Yeah! Oh fuck yes!" screamed Dennys, writhing around in pleasure on her bed. "Thanks for reenacting that one last time for me, Jon."

The two of them sat on Dennys's bed aboard the HMS *Dragonmilf* en route to the Strip. After the amazing courage and heroism that Dennys displayed when rescuing Jon's group from the zombos, he'd felt obligated out of politeness to bend the knee to her.

Beerion was watching in secret from behind a thumb tack when the two began to kiss. Just wanting to spy on the political drama and not on their intimate relations in a perverted way (although that's not to say this wasn't exactly the sort of situation that would get Beerion's rocks off), Beerion went prone and crawled out underneath the closed bedroom door to leave them be.

The two began to undress each other. Dennys removed Jon's armor, his tunic, his pants, and his shirt. Jon removed Dennys's three-dragon pin, her three-dragon logo jacket, her "Draggin, Dragun, and Jragon" monogrammed pants, her triple dragon ring, her "I've Got Three Dragons, Bitch!" hat, her plain white shirt (on which she had drawn her three dragons), and her underwear with "Fire Breathing Dragon (×3)" embroidered on the front.

"Oh yeah . . . sorry about Draggin," said Jon. "I guess you'll have to get some new gear." Dennys began to weep. Jon tried to cheer her up. "You know two dragons isn't so bad, Dennys. In my opinion, two dragons is actually the perfect amount. Two dragons is way cooler than three."

"My dragons are my only children," said Dennys. "I will never bear another child."

Jon wondered if Dennys meant she was choosing not to have other children or if she was literally incapable of becoming pregnant. Jon suspected it was the latter, and this made him very erect.

Dennys looked at the man she did not know was her nephew. "Maybe you can make it up to me by putting your dragon inside me?" She giggled at her joke.

"I'm going to put a dragon inside you," said Jon in a dead serious tone.

Dennys giggled again. Jon began to kiss her.

"I'm going to put a dragon in you," he repeated just as seriously before.

I really want to have sex with Jon, thought Dennys. *But he seems to be taking my joke really seriously in a weird way.*

"Look at me," said Jon, holding Dennys's face in his hands. "I," he said pointing to himself, "am going to put a dragon in you."

"Do you want to just have sex already?" asked Dennys.

"I thought you'd never ask," said Jon, suave as ever. "I guess I can just put a dragon in you later."

Interesting, thought Dennys, confused but ready to have sex with her nephew.

As they laid next to each other on her bed, an idea occurred to Dennys that excited her too much not to mention.

"Wanna try something to really turn me on?"

"Duh," snorted Jon.

"Can you make . . . *it* bend the knee to me?"

"My penis?"

"Oh yeah," said Dennys, moaning at the mere thought of it.

"What does that mean?"

"You know, just like make it sort of kneel and pledge allegiance to me."

"Like, you want me to bend my penis so it looks like it's kneeling to you and then do a voice for it and have it swear loyalty to you?"

"Can you?"

"I can do the voice, but I definitely won't be able to bend my penis in half right now."

They bickered for almost an hour until eventually they found a workable compromise. Finally, Jon had sex for the second time ever while having incest for the first time ever.

⁕

After taking the wheel and making a rocky parallel-parking job in the King's Landing Strip docks, Jon got off the ship. "Land ho!" he shouted for the tenth time that morning.

They were headed to the dragonpit where Cervix had scheduled the meeting to take place.

"Dragonpit ho!" shouted Jon, skipping and whistling and clicking his heels together in midair.

"Very good. That's enough now, Dough," said Beer-ion, massaging his temples.

"Meeting to show Cervix a zombo and have her help us fight the White Wieners ho!" Jon shouted as they began marching to the dragonpit.

Beerion took a long swig from his flask.

Outside the castle walls, the entirety of the Funsullied arranged themselves in one large circle.

"What in the fuck is that?" asked Ser Lemme Bangsister from atop the castle wall.

"Ser, it appears they're trying to intimidate us," replied LeBronn.

"Hit it!" shouted Dog Shit, leading the Funsullied. Suddenly the circle began to spin. Then, over the horizon came thousands of horses being ridden by the Clothkhaki. Into the spinning circle rode Clothkhaki men, whooping and hollering.

"LeBronn, surely they can't fit all their horses in that spinning circle? How are they even entering if its spinning?" asked Lemme, somewhat enraged.

"Easy, Lemme," assured LeBronn. "Don't let it get to you."

But one by one, each Clothkhaki on his horse rode into the circle and kept riding around inside. The men began to pick up the Funsullied from the human perimeter and hoist them onto their shoulders. Now only half the Funsullied stood forming the circle, as the other half balanced on the shoulders of the riding Clothkhaki.

"What are they going to do with the rest of the Funsullied?" asked Lemme. LeBronn was silent. "LeBronn, I asked you a question! What are they going to do?"

What they did was grab the remaining men and balance not one, not three, but two men on each of their shoulders as they rode in increasingly complex patterns with their horses. First it was abstract shapes that looked beautiful, but then they began to spell out letters with the riders: *S-U-C-K O-U-R H-O-L-E-L-E-S-S B-U-T-T-S.*

As they spelled this, the Funsullied began to do impressive acrobatics from atop the shoulders of the Clothkhaki, such as backflips and jumping onto other horses at the same time and perfectly switching places.

Lemme couldn't take it anymore. He stormed away.

"Where are you going?" asked LeBronn.

"To consult the Royal Choreographer," said Lemme.

LeBronn rushed down to meet Jon and his posse as they entered the dragonpit. Their party was quite large. Not in terms of numbers but certainly in terms of the quantity of important characters. Jon stood with Beerion, the Clown, Yora, Peeon, Brian of Fart, Godsdick, a few randoms who inserted themselves into the group by saying they were "friends of the author," and, curiously enough, not Dennys Grandslam. The Clown hauled the chained-up zombo in a box that they'd brought to show Cervix.

LeBronn made a beeline for Godsdick and gave him a great big hug to get his guard down and then punched him in the balls. "What's the matter Gods? Your magic cock can't withstand a good ol' nut tap?"

When he was done wheezing and barfing, Godsdick put his arm around LeBronn and gave him a smile.

"Now how about we leave the adults to their talking and you and me grab a drink?" asked LeBronn.

"That sounds fantastic," said Godsdick.

LeBronn smiled and kicked Godsdick in the nuts again. "Never let your guard down!" he yelled, chuckling. "Now let's get that drink! This round's on you."

LeBronn picked his old squire up off the ground and carried him away.

Jon and the rest took their seats in the empty dragonpit. Suddenly a noise began in the distance.

"Bang-sis-ters! (Hoo!) Bang-sis-ters! (Hah!) Bang-sisters! (Hoo!) Bang-sis-ters! (Hah!)"

The chant grew louder and louder, until Lemme Bangsister entered the dragonpit, leading his sister and their cronies, chanting and clapping and marching. They continued the chant until their whole party was in the arena, at which point they began to do a group dance. Lemme danced proudly and gracefully in front while the rest tried to follow his lead in clumsy unison. Most of them just stood still and looked around, unable to remember the new dance moves Lemme had explained to them just a few moments ago. After thirty seconds of dancing, Lemme gathered everyone in a big clump and went "Bangsisters on three! Bangsisters on three! One... two...three...Bangsisters!" to which a couple people in the group joined in and unenthusiastically said "Bangsisters" along with him. Lemme stuck his hands in the air and twinkled his fingers.

Yourmoms Playboy of the Ironic Islands stood up, took a swig of ale, and smashed the bottle on his head. "Is that my little cousin Peeon?"

"Leave me alone, cousin," pleaded Peeon.

"I didn't know they allowed little bitches in the dragonpit," said Yourmoms. He walked up to Peeon and took a disgusting dead raven out of his pocket that stunk so bad that everyone in the dragonpit held their noses shut. Yourmoms took a blank scroll from the dead raven and said, "This raven's got a letter! For you! I'll read it! 'Dear Peeon, I'm so happy to be severed from you because I am getting more action than I ever did when I was attached to your body. Sincerely, Your Penis. P.S. What are you supposed to be? Some kind of bitch or something?'"

"Really?" asked Peeon holding his nose shut. "Was that joke worth carrying a dead raven and making yourself smell disgusting?"

"Cousin, I'm sorry that your penis wrote such an awfully mean letter to you. But you should thank me for relaying it to you." Yourmoms gave his cousin a wet willy and then sat down next to Cervix. "He doesn't have a penis," he whispered to Cervix, explaining his clever joke.

Cervix stood up. "Now we've got business to attend to, and I really didn't plan this meet-up so we could engage in old interfamily squabbles, so why don't we—"

"Brother!" shouted the Clown, standing up and looking at Ser Greggy. "Is that you, you ugly bastard you? You massive dirty fuck! I've got a familial score to settle with this one!"

Cervix began cursing under her breath and sat down. She took a big sip of wine straight from the bottle.

Ser Greggy, "The Building," grunted back at his brother.

"Are we all done now?" asked Cervix. "Anymore old scores to settle?"

Jon locked eyes with Sideburn and glared at him. Sideburn glared back. For ten seconds they locked eyes until

151

they realized they had never met before and had no beef and stopped glaring at each other.

"Fantastic," said Cervix. "Now, where is the so-called Spider Lady?"

Sideburn quickly whispered into her ear.

"I mean Dragon Queen," said Cervix. "Where's the Dragon Queen?"

"She took her own form of transportation here," said Jon, hiding a smug grin.

Cervix turned red, outraged to have been snubbed by Dennys. "Get on with it then. What's so important that you had to show me?"

The Clown hauled their large chained-up box into the center of the dragonpit. One by one he removed the locks. Finally, he removed the top from the box and took a few precautionary steps backward from the horror that lay inside.

"Surprise!" shouted Dennys, popping out of the box, scaring Cervix so much that she did a spit take with her wine.

"Alright, laugh it up!" shouted an embarrassed Cervix as Dennys high-fived her friends, all of whom had burst into laughter. Beerion was in stitches. He took out a hundred golds, gasping for breath, and handed them to Dennys.

"I can't believe that worked!" Beerion said, doubled over. "I'm crying. I'm actually crying."

"How long were you in that box?" asked Lemme.

"Eight hours!" shouted Dennys, pumping her fists.

"What?" asked Lemme.

"Was this all some joke?" asked Cervix. "Or do you actually have something to show me?"

"You bet my sweet ass I do." Dennys whistled and spoke a command in high Ovarian: "*Come'here-ys!*"

Dragun and Jragon descended into the dragonpit from the sky, each hoisting a rope in his mouth and carrying the real chained-up zombo box. The two dragons dropped the box into the dragonpit and then began to do lap after lap of the arena. Jragon and Dragun flew faster and faster, doing flips and tricks, gliding with ease. The sound of "oohs" and "aahs" echoed off the walls, as for most this was their first time seeing a dragon. The creatures landed and shot beams of fire upward into the sky, screeching as loud as they could.

Wow, I'm really lucky that they decided to do this meet-up in the dragonpit, thought Dennys. *If they had held this literally anywhere else I couldn't have done that really intimidating dragon stuff. I mean, what are the odds that they'd hold the meeting for me, the Dragon Queen, in the pit they have that's designed specifically for dragons? Seems like a dumb move on their part, honestly.*

The Clown took the real zombo box and unchained it. Out popped the zombo, at this point practically just a skeleton with little bits of hair and skin hanging off. The Clown held it by chains as it tried to sprint straight at Cervix and the Bangsister royals.

"Behold," said Jon, "a zombo." Jon threw a banana peel on the ground. The zombo slipped and fell, collapsing on itself into a pile of bones. "Is he dead?" asked Jon. "He's just a pile of bones now. Not scary, right?" Seconds later, the bones reassembled themselves back into their original form, and the zombo kept trying to sprint toward the humans. "Wrong. He's not dead," said Jon, tossing another banana peel. Again the zombo slipped and fell and then reassembled itself. "The zombos will never stop," he said, tossing yet another couple banana peels on the ground. "No matter how many times you deliver a blow," he said, throwing several banana peels directly at the zombo this time, "they will always get back up." By this point Jon had dropped almost a dozen banana peels on the ground. Whoremund continued scarfing down bananas at an uncomfortable clip and tossing his peels to Jon. The zombo was caught in an endless loop of slipping on the peels, collapsing into a pile of bones, reassembling itself, and then slipping again in the giant pile of banana peels. "This is an enemy who doesn't obey kings or queens. This is an enemy who wants chaos and death." Jon pulled a lever that dumped a barrel filled with hundreds of banana peels onto the zombo, burying it. Within seconds the zombo had dug its way out.

"The only way to kill them is to burn them or to shoot them with this: a gunne." Jon held up the ancient weapon for them to see. Jon pushed the zombo onto the ground, loaded his gunne, and fired it into a rag he'd dipped in oil, which caused the rag to combust and burn the zombo, killing it. "So what do you say, Cervix? Will you help us fight the undead? Will you save the human race?"

"Huh, whuh?" Cervix jolted awake. "Oh, you're done. Sorry. Fell asleep for a second there. Um, yeah, so I actually have like twelve of those things in my dungeon already. So, no. I won't help you fight them."

Yourmoms Playboy stood up, mad with indignation. "Ladies and Gentlemen, I've never been scared in my whole life. Not once." He paced back and forth in the center of the pit. "To be honest, I've never even known what fright is supposed to feel like. Is it similar to when you're bored? Or is it like when you're grossed out by something? My whole life I've had no idea. To me, Halloween is like any other day of the week." He pointed at the zombo's ashes. "But this! This monster! This scares the dickens out of me. My pants? Soaked with my own pee right now. My pants? Also soaked with my own shit right now. I want my mom. I'm terrified. And for that reason, I'm going home to the Ironic Islands so I can hide from these scary, scary monsters like a coward. An *honest*, virtuous, brave coward. Good-bye."

And just like that, Yourmoms Playboy walked out of the dragonpit and took off, only stopping briefly to give a few wedgies to Peeon on the way out. If Lemme's head wasn't made of gold, he'd have smiled, watching his sister's suitor cower in fear while he stood strong by her side. Instead, he held the same expression that was permanently sculpted into his gold face (raised eyebrows and a wide open mouth).

"I won't help you fight," said Cervix. "But after seeing my boyfriend, Yourmoms, get frightened to that degree, I will call a truce. Until the war with the undead is over, we will cease fighting with you. For you see... I have a reason to listen to fear again. A reason to cling to the world of the living and stave off death. I am with child." Gasps erupted from everyone in the crowd except Lemme. "Yourmoms just got me pregnant with a 100 percent incest-free child, much like all of my past children who have been robbed from me by the icy, wicked hands of death. Again I reiterate, Yourmoms, a person to whom I am not even tangentially related, is the father of my child. For the love of the Gods, I bet most of you didn't even know he existed until now, which is why I am confident you all believe our love is strong and true. To be clear: none of my siblings got me pregnant this time; nor have they *ever*, least of all Lemme, who, I *suggest*, should stop rubbing my belly and whispering, 'Don't worry, papa's here,' while I am saying all of this."

"Oh wow!" said Dennys, sarcastically. "Thank you soooo much. A truce? That is such a big help in our war against the undead."

Cervix, who didn't understand sarcasm, was flattered. "Why of course. Any good queen would do the same."

"Oh yes," continued Dennys, sarcastically. "You are a great and mighty queen. It's soooo helpful that you won't be actively trying to kill us while we fight undead soldiers to save the human race." She nudged Jon to join in with her.

Jon, who also did not understand sarcasm, tried his best to replicate what it seemed like Dennys was doing.

In the most high-pitched voice he could muster, Jon said, "While I am not as pleased with your decision as Dennys seems to be, I am at least glad that you have called a truce, although I would have preferred that you helped us fight the zombos and the White Wieners."

Well, Jon and Cervix are just great at sarcasm, thought Dennys. *Not!* She smiled the whole way back to Wintersmells, feeling pretty great about herself.

The Nighty Night King

Dawn broke as the Nighty Night King finished kissing each of his zombos goodnight. He replayed the moment when he had killed Dennys's dragon in his head. He rewound and fast-forwarded the part where the spear shot through the dragon's chest, and it really grossed him out. Then he replayed the same thing in slow motion, then a few times really fast; then he added in some special effects; then he inserted a killer soundtrack and then some funny sound effects. *Ewww*, thought the Nighty Night King. The spear ripping through the dragon was really nasty, but he noticed a certain beauty in the dragon as it fell out of the sky in a flurry of air horns, Wilhelm screams, studio audience laughter, sick flames, and greenscreen shots of outer space and the Bahamas. *Boy, I wish I had one of those dragons*, thought the Nighty Night King.

A White Wiener burst through the tent flaps, interrupting the Nighty Night King's tea party with the action figures who were too scared to sleep. "Mr. Nighty Night King, sir—there's something at the frozen lake you need to see *now*!"

The Nighty Night King grew worried. Who would stir Percival the Polar Bear's three sugars just the way he liked it, with the pink flower spoon? The White Wiener dragged the Nighty Night King out of his tent as he cried and reached for his action figures. When they reached the lake the Nighty Night King was fuming, his mascara smeared all over his face. "Someone better be dying, or you guys better have pulled the dragon out of the lake so I can revive it, or so help me ..."

The White Wiener led the Nighty Night King to the frozen lake, where the dragon was laying in pieces. The Nighty Night King stared at the "dragon," which looked like several piles of torn-up flesh covered in barnacles.

"Myself and some of the zombos pulled the dragon out of the lake, sir. We thought maybe you could use your magic to revive ..."

"This pile of dragon parts? How did this happen?"

"Well, sir, the zombos had a lot of trouble attaching their hooks to it. They pulled a piece of it off, then they got mad at each other for doing that, then they pulled even harder and tore off more pieces, and, well ..."

"Nothing a little elbow grease can't fix," said the Nighty Night King. He walked around the piles of dragon parts until he found the dragon's head. It was beautiful: no eyes, skull exposed, eels living in its nose, scales being actively eaten by hordes of seagulls. *Just like in the stories*, thought the Nighty Night King, a tear in his eye.

Wasting no time, the Nighty Night King ran to his tent and slept so he could deal with the dragon in the morning. When he woke up, he returned to the dragon head and stood before it, warming his arms up for the resurrection spell. The Nighty Night King then lifted his hands in the "raise the roof" motion that had become so familiar to him. He waited expectantly for the dragon to wake up. Annoyed, he raised the roof again. Still nothing. He raised it again, and again, and again. He was raising it harder and faster than he ever had before. If there had been a roof above his head, it surely would have been on fire.

But still nothing happened. Dejected, the Nighty Night King fell on the ground and applied his mascara, knowing that he was about to cry. He looked up at the dragon head, admiring how beautiful the seagull eggs in its mouth looked in the sunlight, and his eyes caught its lips. The Nighty Night King wailed and wailed. He cried as hard as he had that time when a zombo made fun of his braces and stole his lunch money, mere seconds ago. He looked at the dragon head once more and brought his face in close to give it one last kiss good-bye. When his puckered lips were just one chest hair away, the dragon sprung to life.

The piles of rotting dragon flesh rolled toward one another and combined in a wet mass. The flesh moved toward the head and attached itself to it, and the dragon's body took form. It looked like a massive, veiny penis with a dragon head on top. The flesh realized this couldn't be right, so it tried again. This time it correctly made the shape of a dragon, but it was inside an absolutely massive, throbbing penis—somehow bigger than before. The flesh kept trying to make a dragon body and succeeded only in making increasingly intricate penises. Finally, after dozens of tries, it managed to make a vagina—a vagina that looked like a penis. The flesh decided to give it one more shot. It tried its hardest to remember what it was like when it was alive—what it felt like to breathe fire, to soar through the skies, to make quiet love to its brothers. As the memories of being a dragon flooded it, the flesh slowly began to take form, to sprout and grow into its former—nope, it was a penis again. This looked like if Leonardo da Vinci drew a penis. This was the *Mona Lisa* of penises.

The Nighty Night King, still standing with his lips puckered and unsure of what to do, ran up to the dragon flesh and kissed it and then ran away. It would probably sort itself out by the time his army had to march on the Trench.

❧

"Trench, ho!" shouted one of the White Wieners, practicing what he would say if he saw the Trench. The zombo army followed the Nighty Night King as he flew atop the reanimated Draggin, which now somewhat resembled a dragon. As they crested a small hill, the army spotted an enormous hole in the distance. It was absolutely terrifying—a gash across the earth with no bottom in sight, a mile wide, cliffs covered in sharp, gnarled rocks. Next to this hole was the Trench, which was much less scary.

"Zombos!" shouted the Nighty Night King as he landed the dragon before the Trench. "Before you lies the Trench. A massive, magical hole created by the First Men to keep us out of the realms of men. Countless beings have died trying to cross it by pole vaulting or attaching balloons to themselves or running at it really fast and jumping. But no more. Today, with the help of our dragon, we will cross the Trench and be one step closer to plunging the world into eternal darkness. Can I get a 'hell yeah'?!"

The zombos were still about a mile away. The Nighty Night King really had flown quite fast. Flustered, he set about trying to figure out how in the world they were going to cross the Trench. He hadn't planned this far ahead.

Maybe Draggin can fly us across one at a time, he thought. *No, no, we're all too fat. I don't want to put a strain on Draggin.* The Nighty Night King plopped onto the edge of the Trench and thought. Then it came to him. His devilish smile returned.

The Nighty Night King stood up and called Draggin over to him. The dragon walked up to the edge—where the Nighty Night King stuck his foot out and tripped it, causing it to fall in. The dragon managed to plug the gap and make a bridge across the Trench. The Nighty Night King was delighted that the plan had worked. Maybe Penelope Peanut would finally forgive him for burning down her doll house because he thought it was a spider the night before.

The zombo army reached the Trench, and the Nighty Night King raised his sword toward the south. "Onward to Westopolis!" he shouted, taking the first steps across the dragon bridge. Almost immediately he tripped and broke his nose. He got up and scrambled across the bridge as the zombos followed, laughing. The Nighty Night King reached the other side and then tripped on nothing and tore his pants. The zombos laughed even harder, and hundreds of them fell off the bridge, their laughter echoing off the cliffs of the Trench and filling the northern air. *When this is over, I'm going to kill myself,* thought the Nighty Night King. *Ow, ow, ow,* thought the dragon as the army stomped across all the penises on its back.

Jon

The castle at Wintersmells finally appeared on the horizon. Jon was relieved to be home. Riding on horseback alongside Dennys—her hair flowing in the wind, his hair assuredly flowing more majestically than hers—things began to feel comfortable again. *Maybe this war against an incalculably massive undead army led by the most formidable adversary we could imagine won't be so bad after all,* Jon thought, smiling. Suddenly, he stopped in his tracks at the sight of his little sister, Malarya. *How many years had it been,* he wondered. *Three? Ten?* This was pointless. His grasp on the concept of time was weaker than ever. Malarya's eyes glistened when she saw him. Jon jumped down from his horse, and the long-lost siblings embraced.

"You used to be taller," Malarya jokingly remarked.

Jon immediately stopped hugging her. "Um…What?" he said, reaching for his sword.

"I was only remarking jokingly," Malarya said nervously.

After a tense few moments, Jon sighed and gave Malarya a smile. "And you used to be shorter," Jon let out and then scolded himself for sinking to dad jokes. He looked Malarya up and down and was relieved to see she was the same as ever, despite the fact that puberty had kicked in hard. He wondered if she had begun to menstruate. *Would it be too weird to ask her?* he thought. *Yeah.* Noticing her sword, he instead said, "You still have it! That fine Ovarian steel."

"Noodle. Its name is Noodle."

"Have you ever used it?"

"Too many times to remember. I've developed a new hobby of killing—it passes the time."

Jon chuckled and ruffled her hair. "I could have used you to protect me. I don't know if you heard, but I died and then was resurrected. Some people are calling me the new Jesus, but, honestly, I'm just happy to be known as 'Jesus.'"

"Um, okay. Well, it is so nice to see you alive. Say, have you reunited with Bland yet?"

"Have you reunited with Bland yet," Jon said, staring at her blankly.

"No, that's not what I meant. That's why I used a comma and a question mark."

"What are you—what? I'm confused."

"Forget it. Let's find him." Malarya shook her head.

The two siblings ventured over to the forest where Bland was staring at a tree. His muscles were bulging out of his shirt, and his face was deadpan.

"I've missed you, Jon," Bland blandly proclaimed while still locking eyes with the tree.

"Brother"—Jon trotted up to Bland and embraced him—"it has been far too long. I have much to tell you of the world!"

"No, you don't. I already know everything," Bland said, this time with even less emotion.

"Okay, great catch-up sesh. You look well. In fact... my Seven Gods, how did your upper body get to be so strong?"

Without batting an eye Bland recited a workout regimen that took forty-five minutes just to describe. He took no pauses and meticulously demonstrated each exercise with proper form as he went through the workout description.

"Jon, are you listening to me?" he said as he finished the last exercise. "You have to keep your arms bent at a right angle or else you won't activate your core properly."

"Mhm, mhm. Well, I have ridden on the back of a dragon, but I suppose that is not interesting to—" Jon's muttering was cut off by Bland.

"I knew you did that. Now, as I was saying, lateral deltoid raises are best accomplished by—Jon, are you listening to me?"

Jon gave him two insincere thumbs-ups, and he and Malarya headed back toward the castle to gossip about how strange Bland was now that he had contracted Pink-Eyed Raven. Meanwhile, Bland wheeled off to a meeting he had scheduled with his new friend Ham, whom he deemed his closest match in brain power. He estimated that Ham was about one-bazillionth as knowledgeable as himself, which far outpaced the one-gazillionth level that the average Wintersmellian possessed. The two nerds had been meeting in the crypt every day for a few weeks now. When they saw each other, they did their new secret handshake, which was just a head bump to signify their brainpower. It would need to be changed soon because they both complained of migraines following their meet-ups.

"He needs to know the truth. Jon isn't really my father's son," Bland announced to Ham. "He's the son of RayRay Grandslam and my aunt, Yomomma Snark. His real name is Eggie Grandslam, and he's the heir to the Pointy Chair."

Ham nodded in agreement. "And we need to tell him before he goes too far with Dennys—they might engage in sexual relations soo—well, actually, in the scheme of things, that's relatively appropriate behavior around here."

"Clap. Clap. Clap," Jon said, his hands full, holding two torches. "Having a secret meeting without me, are you?"

"Jon! It is so great to see you!" Ham bolted up and gave Jon a warm bear hug, making Jon drop the torches into a pool of oil, sending that corner of the crypt up into flames. Hours later in the Wintersmells ICU Burn Ward, they continued their conversation.

"Jon, I knew you'd come find us sooner or later. It's time to have the talk," Bland announced in a fatherly voice.

"I've had sex before—I know how it works. I know what a penis is, okay? It's like a sword between your legs. Also, you're younger than me and much weirder now."

"Jonathan, this talk isn't about you having sex. It's about your parents having sex. I need to tell you who your parents are. Deaddard 'Iron Neck' Snark raised you as his bastard, but your mama is actually Yomomma and your daddy is RayRay Grandslam. You are the rightful Protector of the Realm."

"Did you just call me Jonathan? Is that my real name? If that's true...Are you saying...No. No, that can't be. I'm my *own* dad?!" Jon shouted in disbelief.

"No. That's an impossible conclusion to draw from what I literally just said." Bland grew impatient.

"But if I'm my own dad, then who are you?!" Jon had never been more confused in his life.

"Again, your dad is RayRay Grandslam. That's the last time I will say it."

"I'm a Grandslam? Ew, that's disgusting because that means I had sex with my cousin!" Jon cried. He began to run around Wintersmells yelling "ewwwww" and shaking his hands everywhere. Bland and Ham chased after him, trying not to cause a scene. Nurse Ronnette, on her smoke break, looked up unamused. By the time they made a loop back to the Burn Ward, they were able to catch up to Jon, who was frantically asking people if they knew of virginity-restoration methods.

"Jon, you didn't have sex with your cousin," Ham declared to relieve him of his distress.

"Uh, yeah, I did, Ham. I know how to have sex. And Dennys and I had the sex."

"Wow, congrats man. That's awesome. But what I'm trying to tell you is that you didn't have sex with your cousin because Dennys isn't your cousin—she's your aunt. RayRay, your father, is Dennys's wise older brother, the one who didn't die via molten gold helmet." Ham looked at Jon, who was trying to follow along, as if he were doing mental math. After a few minutes, something clicked in Jon's brain.

"I get it now. Dennys is my aunt. Oh my god! I had sex with my aunt! That's so cool!" Jon took off again for a lap around Wintersmells, this time giving passersby high fives and fist-pumping into the air every few feet as if he were expecting a freeze frame.

"Jon! Dough! Jon Dough!" Jon chanted as people gave him confused looks. One person, Rickety Snark, joined in, but Jon could care less because he didn't know who that was.

"Wanna know something cool?" Jon asked a man shoveling coal.

"Yes, my lord," the man responded automatically.

"I HAD SEX WITH MY AUNT!!"

"Very cool, indeed, my lord."

Jon spent the rest of the afternoon skipping around, reveling in the news of his amazing feat. After a few hours, he began to understand the gravity of the new information. *It's really, really cool that I had sex with my aunt*, Jon thought to himself. He also realized that this meant he was the rightful heir to the Pointy Chair. *Hmm, that thought of mine rhymed*, Jon chuckled to himself.

He stumbled upon a pond in the forest and saw his reflection in the shiny water. No longer did the face that greeted him belong to a bastard. He saw himself for the first time as a Grandslam, a true highborn. But he regarded himself as so much more than that: he was also the coolest guy around because he fucked his aunt!

⚜

Later that day, Dennys led Jon to the field where Dragun and Jragon were feeding on cattle. The two creatures were surrounded by hundreds of pig skeletons and horse carcasses. Beside these skeletons stood hundreds and hundreds of live pigs, horses, goats, elephants, and chickens, all waiting in tow to be eaten. Jon couldn't even make out any grass due to the carpet of feeding scraps.

"They've hardly had anything to eat!" Dennys exclaimed. "I hope they'll survive!"

Jon gave another look around to see if he had confused the immense supply of food for something else. No, he had seen correctly the first time. The dragons then turned to stare right at Jon and began growling.

Dennys motioned to Jon and said, "Give it to them."

He looked down. She was pointing at the small turkey leg in his hand. "They have so many live, very large animals here. Why do they need my small piece of meat?" Jon pleaded. Dennys crossed her arms and furled her brow at Jon. "Okay! Okay, just one second." He went to take one last bite, but Dragun darted at him and snatched the turkey leg from his hand. "I am so hungry," Jon said quietly.

Then he remembered the few saltine crackers he had stashed in his pocket from the tavern a few towns ago. He began unwrapping their packaging. The dragons growled louder, and Dennys motioned, this time more dramatically, to his crackers. "No. Please, this is my *only* food. They have so so so much food. Please." Dennys crossed her arms again.

Jon put his head down and held the crackers out. Dragun licked them off his hand and then spit them out, not perfectly content with their level of salt.

"Now that they are fed, we ride." Dennys walked over to them and hopped on Dragun's back. "Well, go on," she called out to him. Jon approached Jragon. Never had he been so close to a veritable beast.

"Okay...Here goes nothing," Jon said timidly. He jumped a few inches in the air and landed in the exact same spot where he was standing.

"You have to mount it!" Dennys cried out annoyed.

"Well, okay...How do I mount it?" As he finished his words, Jragon picked Jon up by the shirt and flung him onto his scaly back. "Oh my god. Oh my god. Okay... Now how do I ride it?"

171

"Oh Jon, you silly goof. Just watch how I do it." She yipped Dragun into motion, and they took to the skies majestically.

Jragon took off, catching up to his brother. Jon fell off almost immediately and plummeted back toward earth. Jragon begrudgingly swooped back down and caught him on his back once more.

"What do I hold onto?" Jon cried.

"Um, maybe the *dragon*," Dennys laughed, twirling through the air on the back of Dragun.

"Oh, no!" Jon cried as he slid off the dragon's back during a sharp turn. "The only thing with any grip on this damn beast is his . . . his—"

To Dennys's surprise, she turned behind her to see her beloved Jragon wincing in pain as Jon dangled below him, grasping his testicles. She made the executive decision to land right then, and she assumed both Jragon and Jon would be relieved.

They descended into a beautiful stretch of luscious grass, complemented with a booming waterfall that fell into a glistening river.

"Don't you just love it out here?" asked Dennys, with a twinkle in her eye. She touched Jon's arm ever so slightly. "The way the crispness of the cool air bites your skin as the scenery fills your mind with epic reminiscences of the beauty of life?"

"To be honest, this type of scenery doesn't really get my dick that hard."

"Hm," Dennys frowned. "You do not need to be so blunt."

"Nah. That's what I'm saying. If you would *listen*, it's not blunt; it's, like, just completely flaccid right now." Jon sighed. He turned toward Dennys in order to avoid the boring scenery and suddenly felt a stirring in his heart. "Dennys, now that I'm looking at you, I must admit you're so much prettier than all these dogshit trees and rivers around us. Like, much, *much* prettier."

Dennys's frown was replaced by a subtle smirk. "Well, Jon Dough, the feeling is mutual, I assure you." She stepped to Jon and grabbed the back of his neck, pulling him down for a kiss. It was only a moment until they had made their way to the ground. And the rest, as they say, is sex.

Throughout the entirety of Jon and Dennys's lovemaking, both dragons locked eyes with Jon while dragging their fingers across their throats, as if to signal that Jon was dead meat. Dragun pounded his fist into his hand, while Jragon mimed ripping a person in half. Dragun mouthed the words "dead man walking." Steam billowed out of their angry ears.

As for Jon, he was just happy to see the dragons getting into it as much as he was.

Just as they were finishing up, Jon said, "I need to tell you something important."

"Do you have an STD? Another family? Does your other family have STDs?!"

"No, no, it's nothing that serious," he reassured her. "Although you may lose all of your power and claim to the throne," he mumbled under his breath.

"What was that?"

"Oh, nothing. I just was saying you look very pretty in the light of Jragon's fire breath."

Jon suddenly became nervous to tell his beautiful Dennys the news. His palms were sweating, his knees felt especially weak, and his arms were heavy. However, on the surface, he looked calm and ready. He gazed into her eyes as if it were the last time, feeling as though things might never be the same between them. Jon took a deep breath and began.

"I love you too," Dennys blurted out just as Jon announced he was a Grandslam and had a claim to the Pointy Chair. "Oh, I thought you were gonna say something different," she despondently uttered.

"I, well...um."

"But how can you be so sure of all this?"

"Bland and Ham both knew."

"So your brother and your best friend told you that you're the rightful heir to the Chair? Checks out!"

"How do you feel about this information?"

"I'm a little weirded out since I'm now learning I just had sex with my cousin...again."

"No, no we're nephew and aunt!"

"Oh, okay. Well, that's still not that cool. That's, like, just about as bad in my eyes—"

"Hell yeah!" Jon yelled, not paying attention. He went in for the high five.

Dennys turned away and brushed her hand through her long blonde wisps. While she descended deep into thought, Jon began daydreaming about how beautiful their children would be, once he was able to convince her that he'd "had a vasectomy." And once you were able to look past the genetic deformities. Dennys would have made a wonderful ruling queen, but think of how great she would be as a homemaker, Jon thought chivalrously.

❧

Up in the Great Hall, the battle against the undead was being drawn up on the strategy table, known in Winter-smells as the "Table of Strategy."

"When I inevitably die, I hope it's from someone big and strong because it would be so embarrassing to be killed by a little wiener," the Clown announced, carefully moving some of the figurines an inch to the left to emphasize his point.

"My dream death tomorrow is for someone to cut off my head and then be disappointed to find out it's already been cut off. And then I'll just stab myself in the chest to show 'em who's boss," Lemme chimed in, adjusting some of the blocks of wood that were supposed to represent one side or the other in the battle.

Beerion had heard enough of this. "If we're gonna die, let's do it the right way! I've always said it, but I'll say it again: I hope to die at the age of eighty with a nice bottle of wine and a girl around my cock. You know what? Scratch that. Make it two girls and just one cup of wine.

But yeah, since I'm probably dying tomorrow, it will be hard to find two girls who are free, so I'll just settle for two cock rings and a warm beer to do the trick." He thought for a moment. "Actually, I'm just going to go masturbate and drink a glass of water."

Everyone reveled in this particular fantasy except Lord Varysectomy. He had always held a different vision regarding his ultimate demise. He dreamed that he would retire to his quarters for the night, open up the secret trap door in his floor, and pull out the large chest he stored there. He would open the chest and out would stumble a man who had not seen the light of day in years, decades perhaps, if he lived long enough. This was the man who had cut off Varysectomy's genitals when he was but two years old. He would grab the man by the chin and force him to meet his eye.

"When I was a boy," Varysectomy would say, "you took my genitals away from me. And now, I'm going to punch you." He would then punch him. After that, Varysectomy would pass away from cancer many years later. *That's* how he wanted to die.

Suddenly, Bland entered the Room of the Table of Strategy and interrupted the conversation. "How can you all think like this? We aren't going to die! We will fight and beat the White Wieners! The fate of the kingdom depends on it at least," Bland said, disappointed.

"I have seen a zombo. And I have heard of their numbers. I am sorry, but how can you believe we have a chance?" asked Brian of Fart.

"Because there's no 'I' in 'team.' Because hard work beats talent when talent doesn't work hard. Because it's not about waiting for the storm to pass—it's about learning to dance in the rain. Also, I have a plan."

"Bland, I'm just gonna remind you that there is a 'me' in 'team,' and there's also a 'meat.' Not sure if that's helpful but just saying," Ham chimed in.

Bland began to wonder if Ham was really as smart as he believed him to be. He shook his head and returned to the matter at hand. "As I was saying, I have a plan to lure the Nighty Night King in and well…it's me. I'm the lure. I'm the Pink-Eyed Raven. He'll want to get his hands on me more than anything. And in case that doesn't work, I'm going to use my biggest strength: my sexuality. Look at my arms. Have you ever seen anyone with more perfect muscle tone? No, you haven't. I just scanned your entire memory bank and can say with certainty that I am the sexiest boy you have ever seen. I'm going to wear my best trench coat with nothing under and spray on a little Chanel #4."

"Oh, Bland!" Pantsa pleaded. "We can't leave you alone out there as bait. You'll be unsafe!"

"I'll protect him," Peon exclaimed as he stood up and saluted. "I too promise to wear a trench coat and go commando in dutiful honor of the living! I swear to stare sexily into that evil king's eyes and lick my lips in the face of death."

"Well, then it's settled!" cried Beerion, wanting to move things along. "There's no need to stress about it now! There is only one thing that we all must do, however—SHOTS! A drink to our sexy Bland! And a drink to the good land of Fart from which our dear Brian hails!"

"To Fart!" they all shouted and chugged their drinks. To onlookers, it would seem that these northern leaders were in for a wild night before the most important battle of their lives—and those onlookers would be right. One moment they were playing a casual game of "Chug the Bottle," and the next they were taking body shots off of the Clown. Beerion swung from chandelier to chandelier to brick wall, laughing all the way.

Lord Varysectomy was so drunk he swore his testicles had grown back. Beerion was so drunk he swore he had grown 300 percent taller. As it happened, Beerion had only climbed into Varysectomy's pocket in order to gain a higher vantage point, dangling like a pair of testicles. Perhaps the most intoxicated person was Lemme. He drank like a mom on her fiftieth birthday turning "thirty-two again." He spent a good part of the night in a headstand to show off the benefits of having a golden head and nearly convinced Brian to cut hers off in solidarity.

At around 2:00 a.m., Beerion climbed up on the table and made an announcement to the group.

"It's time to get serious, everyone. We have an imminent battle where we must show the dead that life wins out. You only live once!" Jon ducked his head and hoped nobody was looking at him. "One more drink for good luck!" Beerion shouted as he threw back another. Standing only as tall as your everyday spoon and weighing no more than a few, erm, spoons, Beerion was a remarkable drinker. Yet this moment was his last memory of the night. He awoke to the sound of Jon's trembling voice.

"The Nighty Night King is coming! And the White Wieners have already arrived! They're not as cute as I was hoping! They actually look very scary! You guysssss?!"

The crowd in the Great Hall started to get up slowly. *What happened last night?* everyone collectively wondered. Pantsa was lying in a pool of vomit. Brian was sitting in a pool of vomit. The Clown stood with vomit surrounding his feet in a pool shape. This battle would be the ultimate hungover walk of shame.

George R. R. Martin

Holy hell, talk about shameful hangovers. It's been—my God, has it really been—no that cannot possibly be right … *Chauncibell! Is this newspaper correct? Is it the twenty-sixth already?* Jesus, George, you've gotta stop ordering double bellinis. *Chauncibell, start whipping up a single. Maybe make two …*

Yes, "Cabo-time" is a real phenomenon. Real as the sun on my face or the constant recurring image of a gnome dueling with a fairy in my head. It's been thirteen days since I have had even one single moment away from officiating over the Cabo-wide limbo contest to read any of this book I've been scratching out. Now, granted, I've yet to proofread anything, but I feel fairly certain that all my concerns from the prologue about misremembering locations' names or major plot points or even the names of the characters were unfounded. Character? *Characters*, right? I must have written in more than *one* person in this book, yeah? Doo doo doo, flip, flip, flip, let's see here, yes, okay, good, *characters*. I think that I am veritably on a roll here, spinning out perhaps some of my best work yet. Maybe not my *best* work. That first book was pretty damn good. But that was before all the money, all the fame. That was a younger, wiser me. Bright-eyed and creative as a . . . oh boy, what the hell is a good simile for something creative? Creative as a . . . Creative like a . . . Fuck it. *Oh, you're too good to me, Chauncibell! You brought the peanuts I like too.*

Based on Chauncibell's feedback, it seems I'm halfway to another best seller. And that means I'm halfway to receiving my best paycheck yet, which in turn means I can afford eight more beautiful months in Cabo. *Yes, Chauncibell. Eight months. Well, frankly I have no conception of what that could possibly be. Your son wants you to be there for his gradua-what? Well, then you can fly him out here to celebrate with both of us. No you can't "at least have that day off."*

So, without too much delay, let's get back to our story. Chauncibell informs me that we left off right before the battle of the living versus the dead. This is a chapter I have written a thousand times in my head. I have been ruminating over the specifics of the battle for years now. This is perhaps the most confident I have ever been before diving in and putting thoughts to the page, inklings to ink. This next chapter is going to be epic, a piece of pure literary gold, and best of all a breeze to write. And if I could just enter the correct password for my HBO login, I would be able to refresh my memory of how this battle is supposed to unfold. Okay, gotta guess my password. How about "DennysRRMartin"? Nope. "GeorgeOfTheRings"? Nope. "LordOfTheRings1"? "GeorgeAndLeBronnForever"? "Alcohol"? None of those, damn. "DeltaChiDelta4Lyfe"? "AceRRMartin"? "ScorpionRRMartin"? "CoolRRMartin"? "George-RRMartin69"? Okay, hold on—this next one has to be it: "GeorgeRRMartin69Blowjob." No?? Okay this next one is definitely it: "GeorgeRRMartin69Blowjob-Handjob." Negative. Okay this next one is 100 percent it: "GeorgeRRMartin69BlowjobHandjobSecks." Whoops, I meant "GeorgeRRMartin69BlowjobHandjobSex." What?! Still no?

No matter! I would never dare use the show to inform my writing of this book, anyway. No, I would never. Never. Unless, "GeorgeRRMartin69BlowjobHandjob-Sex1" is correct? Nope. So, then, let's see. I can still do this the old-fashioned way—just gotta get my creative juices flowing. What time do we think it is there in Wintersmells? And what would it feel like there in the air? Let's really set the scene. *No, Chauncibell, I am not stalling because I don't have any idea how to start the battle. Stop reading over my shoulder. Yes, you are paid by the task. No, bellinis do not count as a task. Making those is a favor you do for me in exchange for my company.* Anyway, I am going to say that it is probably night in Winter-smells. And the air is crisp. Voluptuously crisp. But not *too* voluptuously crisp.

Malarya

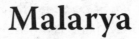

The night air outside Wintersmells was voluptuously crisp. *Too* voluptuously crisp. On all sides the castle was surrounded by what seemed like an infinite wall of zombos and White Wieners. Of course it only *seemed* infinite. An infinite number of anything is impossible. And I would not want to tarnish the plausibility of this series on a simple numerical hyperbole. Death had come knocking on the door of the living, and the living couldn't pretend like they weren't home because they'd accidentally said, "Who is it?" instead of looking through the peephole—metaphorically, that is. Though the personification of death is a most enjoyable thing, again, I'm just looking out for the plausibility here. The fate of humanity rested on the shoulders of the motley crew of outsiders, outcasts, weirdos, magicians, stars of this series, and janitors who laid in wait inside the walls of Wintersmells.

It's killin' time, thought Malarya as she said "It's killin' time" out loud.

The army of the living assembled outside the gates, laying eyes on the ungodly horde of zombos in the distance. Twenty minutes later, once everyone had finished changing into new pants, they assembled once again. Malarya stood in the front, riding her gunne like a horse and dancing around.

"Who's ready to die?" shouted Malarya, causing several different young Snark soldiers to throw up and start crying. "This gunne is my dick, and I'm going to fuck these zombos in the mouth!" Malarya looked into the distance and noticed something so somber that it caused her to put down her gunne penis and stop dancing: it was her brother Bland, dressed in a leather bikini top, cutoff jean shorts with the pockets hanging out and the word "fancy" printed on the butt, and high-heel stilettos. His face was covered in red mascara and lipstick. All of it to attract the Nighty Night King. Peeon pushed Bland in his wheelchair toward the weirdwood tree where he would wait as the sexy boy bait. In that moment, Malarya realized that Bland, cowering in a chair, dressed as a dime-store hooker, was the bravest person she knew.

The battle was imminent. *Yip Yip Yip!* called out the Clothkhaki phalanx, not realizing that their war cry wouldn't work this time because zombos are incapable of being disturbed by annoying sounds. Regardless, they were ready to give their lives for humanity. The Clothkhaki had made peace with their gods. Though, as they rode forward, some began to wonder if they had almost certainly been praying to the wrong gods the whole time, seeing as all the other characters consistently received magical help from their gods—being brought back to life, setting things on fire, healing, and the like... They would think about this later, they thought.

"*CHARGE!*" shouted the Clothkhaki commander, "charge" being Clothkhaki for "attack." Off went the entire population of the Clothkhaki on their horses, galloping into darkness as the first line of attack for the humans. Who better to fight the undead than the most alive, animalistic, passionate, instinctive, impulsive, stupid army on the planet? The Clothkhaki stampeded right toward the enemy with weapons in their hands and no battle plan or strategy in their minds whatsoever.

"So these huge strong Clothkhaki guys are going to take care of this for us, right?" asked one of the youngest Snark soldiers to the rest of the army. "Like, they're going to kill everyone and we won't actually have to fight magically enchanted undead corpses?"

An elder Snark soldier chuckled and looked down at the quivering young lad. "If you'd seen what I saw the Clothkhaki do decades ago at the battle of Tacoboat, you wouldn't be worried one bit."

But as the Clothkhaki got further and further away from the castle, their *yips* turned into *yeoows* and then finally into silence as the zombos quickly exterminated their whole army.

"You are going to die tonight, son," said the elder soldier, driving a sword through his own neck. The young soldier left to go change his pants again.

Fuck, thought Malarya. *Those zombos just killed the entire Clothkhaki population. Isn't that genocide, technically? I mean, I know the zombos are trying to wipe out all humans, which is definitely very evil, but it still feels messed up, even for them, to commit a genocide.*

Ser Boats prepared to send the next squad of men, this time Snark fighters, out to certain death. But suddenly, in the nick of time, he no longer had to, because certain death was coming straight toward them. The Nighty Night King pointed toward Wintersmells, and the zombos followed, charging at the humans by the thousands. With the zombos gone, the Nighty Night King checked to make sure the coast was clear and then took out his binoculars to get a quick little glimpse of Bland over at the weirdwood tree.

Malarya couldn't help but smile as the zombos came running toward her. "It's killing time, still."

Pantsa jumped into action immediately, leaving the battleground to go hide with the women and children.

"Oh, well this is disgusting," Pantsa remarked upon arriving in the cellar with the mothers protecting their kids. "I'm going to uh, go . . . back to the battle," she lied. Pantsa left and went to a separate, much fancier cellar she'd constructed just for this sort of occasion.

"Phew," whispered Lord Varysectomy to Beerion, both of whom were wearing dresses and wigs to blend in with the women. "Looks like she didn't notice us."

Back on the battlefield, things were heating up. "Did somebody order a lead sandwich?" quipped Malarya, shooting a zombo in the head. She quickly turned and shot another zombo right between the eyes. "Tell the missus you're gonna be home a little late tonight!" Then another. "Have you met my gunne? She has something she wants to say to you!" Another zombo dead. "Time flies when you're having *gunne*!" Then two zombos dead with one shot. "Two for one without a coupon? Now *that's* a deal!" Then Malarya shot a very tall zombo in the genitals, and it spun around and made a fart sound when it collapsed. *I swore I had a line for this exact situation*, thought Malarya, staring at the corpse, trying really hard to think of the quip. "Swirly dirly fart, you tall...fuck? Is that something? What's the line? It definitely had 'dirly' in it..."

Meanwhile Ham Tardy was trying his best to survive the devastating swarms of the undead. "I killed a White Wiener once! I killed a White Wiener once!" he shouted as he spun in circles, trying to avoid zombos. Finding himself surrounded and unable to run, Ham continued to uselessly spin in circles until he slipped and fell. "Don't step any closer! I read about your kind in a book!" he said from the ground, momentarily out of reach of the zombos.

"Apologies, Ser Lemme!" shouted Brian of Fart, who'd showed up just in time to save Ham. Hoisting Lemme as a battering ram, she smashed his gold head through the zombos and killed each one of them. Ham was saved.

"It's actually way harder to kill a White Wiener than a zombo," he said, getting up and brushing a mixture of both his own feces and random feces off of his clothes. "They're much higher-ranking officers in the undead army. I killed one once." As the words came out of his mouth, Ham discovered a brilliant new strategy for his fighting. He promptly ran to hide behind a thin tree and let everyone else kill the zombos for the rest of the battle.

All around Malarya, the living were being completely overwhelmed by the undead. She watched as human soldiers were chomped up, pulled apart, and even slashed to pieces by the screeching, relentless zombos.

"*Help!*" they yelled.

"*Save me!*" they pleaded.

But Malarya was too busy doing 360-degree backflips, shooting zombos midair, and then shouting, "Talk about *flipping the script*!" to worry about saving her lousy fellow soldiers. Could she have saved countless lives if she wasn't spending extra time doing cool tricks with her gunne and saying awesome quips after each kill? Probably. But killing zombos wasn't as fun as killing humans, and as she'd been reminded several times, there were no humans in this battle that she was allowed to kill, so she had to spice things up somehow.

Suddenly a fist came swinging at Malarya. She dodged just in time and saw who the fist belonged to.

"The Clown?" she asked.

"Little girl!" said the Clown, realizing he'd almost hurt the only person on the planet he didn't actively despise. "I didn't realize that was you. I've sort of been killing anything that moves out here. Zombos, humans, horses, you know how it goes."

"No fair!" shouted Malarya. "Can I join?"

The Clown kicked her to the ground. "You rascal! Not this time." And just like that, the Clown hopped on a horse and rode off, punching the horse as hard as he could.

"Aw, man," pouted Malarya, somberly returning to fighting. She was so bummed out that she could only muster the enthusiasm to do a 180-degree flip before shooting the first zombo she saw.

On a hilltop overlooking the battle, Jon and Dennys prepared the Wintersmells air force.

"Giddy-up!" said Jon as he mounted Jragon, prompting an angry screech from the beast.

"Jon!" whispered Dennys. "In the high Ovarian tongue, 'giddy-up' means something very, very offensive. Do not say it around the dragons." She leaned in and whispered, "Especially Jragon." Dennys mounted Dragun and took to the skies as Jon followed close behind.

"*Dracarys*!" shouted Jon, which caused his dragon to do nothing.

"Huh?" said Dennys. "What's that you just said? *Dracarys*? What in the seven hells is that even supposed to mean, Jon? That's the dumbest piece of gibberish I've ever heard."

"Sorry, what's the fire command?"

"*Gasolina.*"

"Oh, right. *Gaaaaa...*"

"*Solina.*"

"Right. *Prasolina.*"

It was close enough. The dragons dove down over the fight, shooting fire onto the battlefield, burning somewhere between a dozen and twelve zombos every second.

"Man," said Jon, "maybe we should've started riding the dragons from the beginning?"

"What do you mean?" asked Dennys, diving down to burn more zombos. "I feel like we chose the right time to come in and turn the tides."

"Yeah, but look at how much damage the dragons are doing against the zombos. We're just vaporizing them. Don't you feel like if we'd gone out from the start, the entirety of the Clothkhaki wouldn't have died? And all the thousands of my men that have died already wouldn't have died?"

"Look, in order for this to be the longest, most cinematic battle sequence of all time, we needed to eat up some time with ground-forces footage. We couldn't just start with the dragons or else—nevermind. You're overthinking this."

Before Jon could shrug and agree with her, Jon and Dennys were startled by the sound of an ear-shattering, ungodly shriek not coming from either of their dragons. It was the Nighty Night King, riding a reanimated Draggin, shrieking at the top of his lungs as his dragon remained silent.

"Draggin?" said Dennys, beginning to tear up. "C'mere boy. Is that you?"

"*Gasolina*!" shouted Jon, shooting a beam of fire at the zombo-fied Draggin.

"Jon, no!" protested Dennys. "Don't hurt my dragon! He's my child!"

"Dennys, it's not actually—"

The Nighty Night King took advantage of the time they were wasting bickering to command Draggin to blast a beam of exotic blue fire at Dennys. Whereas red fire is hot, blue fire is blue.

Not one to let someone hurt his queen, Jon attacked the Nighty Night King with fire once again. Dennys saw Jon attacking Draggin and was outraged that he wasn't listening to her. Not one to let someone hurt her dragons, she turned to Jon and started shooting fire at him. The Nighty Night King noticed Dennys blasting Jon with fire, Jon blasting him with fire, and no one blasting Dennys with fire. Not one to let an enemy be the only person not getting blasted with fire, the Nighty Night King unleashed a steady stream of fire blast right on Dennys.

After a full minute of futile triangular fire blasting, the Nighty Night King hopped off Draggin and made a mad dash on foot for Bland and the weirdwood tree. Jon followed in hot pursuit, making his way to the ground and sprinting after him.

"Jon!" shouted Dennys. "You're much more helpful and effective in this fight on a dragon. Come back!"

"No, I got this!" he replied mid-sprint. "I really, *really* want to kill this guy myself!"

Hearing him, the Nighty Night King turned around and locked eyes with Jon. Surrounded by piles of fallen soldiers, the Nighty Night King raised his arms in the all-too-familiar "raise the roof" motion, but he didn't stop there. He took his raised arms to the left, then to the right, his hips following with all their might. He started to pull his arms behind him and simultaneously threw his pelvis forward. He stuck his arms out as if he were driving a car and dropped his ass low, wiggling it left and right behind him. He was bumping and grinding, getting lower than low. Then the Nighty Night King dropped his hands to the floor and shook that ass up and down so hard that it could've caused an earthquake.

What followed was the most powerful resurrection of dead men into zombos that the Nighty Night King had ever summoned. It wasn't just the thousands of recently dead soldiers who immediately stood up with blue eyes and began attacking Jon. Every dead body in every cemetery in the whole North heeded the Nighty Night King's call, crawling out of its grave and sprinting toward Jon Dough, no matter how many days the journey would take.

"Dennys?" panicked Jon. "Dennys, you were right! This was a mistake!" he shouted, though Dennys, Jragon, and Dragun were miles in the air.

Meanwhile, the battle was raging on, and hope was slowly vanishing for the humans. The zombos had overwhelmed them so thoroughly that they'd been forced to retreat to safety inside the walls of Wintersmells, which were then immediately breached by the zombos. Malarya was as giddy as the schoolgirl she would've been if not for the atrocious parenting from an extremely violent man whose beheading she witnessed. She'd just invented the phrase "cowabunga" after she'd thrown a zombo dozens of feet into the air and then shot it in the genitals. When she opened her mouth afterward, the celebratory phrase instinctively came out, and she had a feeling that it was really going to take off.

As Dennys tried to wipe out the hordes of zombos on Dragun, she once again ran into zombo-fied Draggin as he flew in front of her, growling and ready to strike.

"Here, boy!" she tried again. "Come to mama!"

Draggin sent blue fire straight at her.

"Okay, easy, boy!" she shouted, narrowly dodging the fire. Dennys was impervious to fire, but *blue* fire? It was anyone's guess if she was impervious to that. "Draggin, it's mom. I know you're still in there. He's put some spell on you, but I am your mother, and I know I can get through to you. The real you," she began to tear up. "Draggin, I love you. I always have, and I always will...no matter what."

Draggin rammed Dennys off of Dragun and then flew over to the castle to burn more stuff.

Dennys woke up on the ground soon after, surrounded by zombos. She had no weapon. It seemed like the end of the line for her. Dennys began to utter what she realized might be her last words.

"I don't love you, Draggin!" she shouted. "I'm not actually your mom! 'Mother of dragons' is just an expression I say! It's not like you have my DNA! I just raised you! And you were the shittiest dragon!"

"Oh, hey, Dennys, funny seeing you here," panted Yora Mormon, rolling in frantically on his wheelchair, which had two swords attached to it. He cut through the zombos as he clumsily wheeled around. "Oh, I guess I'm sort of saving you right now, haha, so random," he said, taking out a dagger and stabbing a zombo right before it bit Dennys. As he killed it, the zombo lightly fell onto Yora, which ripped open his soft skin and caused his innards to spill out. "Cowabunga!" shouted Yora. "That's a cool new phrase young kids are using. You say it when something hurts, right?" Yora collapsed onto the ground.

"Yora! You're hurt!" Dennys said.

"Ah yes, I suppose I'm going to die now. A small price to pay to save my queen. At least I get to say good-bye with a . . . *tender kiss*."

"Oh . . . um, thank you so much for saving me," said Dennys uncomfortably. "I've got to go fight now. I will . . . miss you terribly."

"Ah yes!" wheezed Yora. "How tragic to say good-bye forever, but it's almost worth it, knowing I'll get one parting kiss from my lovely queen."

"Uh huh," she said, purposely ignoring him as she took the swords off his wheelchair for herself. "You were a great guy, Yora. Great life. Going to be missed for sure."

"And it's with a farewell in the form of a pressing of your lips against mine that I will feel safe going into the darkness that is death."

"Uhhhhh, okay, fine, here's your farewell kiss," she said, leaning in. As Yora shut his eyes and made a kissing face, Dennys silently tiptoed away, blew Yora an air kiss, and ran back to the battle. Yora died thirty minutes later with his lips puckered, still thinking she was about to kiss him.

Over at the weirdwood tree, the Nighty Night King arrived to eliminate humanity's last Pink-Eyed Raven. Bland began his plan to distract him.

"Whoopsie-daisy," said Bland, dropping his bikini top and feigning that it was an accident. The Nighty Night King's lips began salivating uncontrollably as he unsheathed his knife. "Did I do that? I'm so silly," said Bland. The Nighty Night King was holding up his knife, but suddenly he was too entranced to strike. Peeon hid behind the weirdwood tree, preparing to attack.

"You got this," Peeon said, psyching himself up. "Just go and kill him." He tried desperately to hold back the tears that welled at the mere notion of violence. "You can apologize to him afterward," he said, slapping himself in the face.

Bland lured the Nighty Night King even closer by rubbing massive amounts of baby oil on his toned biceps.

"Could anyone spot me while I do some pull-ups on this tree branch?" asked Bland. "I *really* need to get my reps in and would be so, *so* grateful." The Nighty Night King couldn't help it. He quickly dropped all notions of murder and volunteered, figuring it was the least he could do. At that moment Peeon popped out with his sword and charged toward the Nighty Night King.

"I'm so sorry about this!" shouted Peeon as he raised his sword and quickly got stabbed by the Nighty Night King, who'd just snapped out of his state of distraction. "Oh goodness, Mr. Nighty Night King, I've gotten my blood all over your knife and your shoes, and I've just tried to ruin your plan to kill Bland. Can you ever forgive me?"

The Nighty Night King cut Peeon's throat and knocked him over.

"Bland," Peeon wheezed, "does this mean we're all good? Your family and me? We're cool? I know I kidnapped you and your brother and killed some of your friends and took over Wintersmells for a minute there, but now that I'm dying to protect you, we're all square, yeah? Bygones are bygones? Right, Bland? We're totally good, you and me? Past is the past? Water under the bridge, Bland? All good? I'm redeemed? Now that I'm going to…" Peeon trailed off and died an honorable death, his character arc coming full circle in an impressively satisfying and neat manner.

The Nighty Night King continued toward Bland, this time not succumbing to his diversions.

"Man, I sure wish I had someone to rub this tanning oil on my lower back," tried Bland. The Nighty Night King continued steadfastly toward him, hellbent on murder. "Could someone help me cut my shorts a little shorter?" asked Bland nervously. Nothing. He was desperate to distract the Nighty Night King. "Uhhhh," he floundered. "I hope no one minds if I just get naked right now," he said. Nope. It was useless. But Bland doubled down. "Yeah, so I guess I'll just get completely naked right about now—"

"Ahhhhhhhh!" shouted Malarya, jumping literally fifty feet into the air and landing on the Nighty Night King from behind, her Ovarian steel dagger in hand. The Nighty Night King turned around and caught her, grabbing her hand before she could stab him.

Nice try, she thought. *I've got you right where I want you.* Malarya dropped the dagger, letting the Nighty Night King think he'd won, and she caught the blade with her other hand. *Hasta la vista, baby*, thought Malarya, inventing another awesome catchphrase as she stabbed the dagger forward. But the Nighty Night King reacted just in time and grabbed her other hand, stopping the knife. *I bet you think you're clever, eh?* she thought, dropping the dagger once again, catching it with the original hand down low.

"Catch *this*," she said, as the Nighty Night King caught it, grabbing her hand before she could stab him once again. *Here goes nothing*, thought Malarya as she dropped the knife yet again, the blade now so low that she had to catch it with her foot. Malarya pretended to stab him with her foot to fake him out, dropped the dagger again, caught it with her other foot, dropped it again, let it land on the ground, picked it up with her other foot, and then kicked the blade into the Nighty Night King's shin. "I guess the *knife* is on the other *shoe*," she quipped, "or wait, no. Looks like the *shoe* is gone and now the *knife* is on the other *foot*—no, no, wait. I got this. Here we go: *Knife* to meet you!"

That was it. The Nighty Night King shattered into dust immediately. Every single zombo and White Wiener dropped dead in an instant.

"I'm gonna kill you, Mr. The Nighty Night King!" shouted Jon, arriving at the weirdwood tree in a sprint, his sword raised above his head. "Where's the—uh, where's the Nighty Night King?"

"Malarya just killed him, Jon," said Bland. Jon entered a state of shock.

"No, but the Nighty Night King!" Jon reiterated. "He's alive, right? I fought my way through thousands of zombos, and now I've come to kill him and end the battle!"

"Jon," said Malarya, "I just killed him. I'm so sorry. I know you really wanted to do it yourself."

Jon's face dropped, and his eyes filled with tears. He let his sword fall to the ground. He was too weak to hold it anymore after hearing the news.

"Oh," he said, his voice cracking, snot coming out of his nose, "that's so awesome Malarya. I'm so proud and happy you did that." That was all Jon could eke out before he began bawling.

From the weirdwood tree, they could hear the ecstatic cheers of the survivors at Wintersmells. The battle was over, and the celebration was about to begin. Malarya and Bland stayed behind to comfort Jon as he fell and curled into a ball. Jon wrapped his arms around himself and rocked back and forth until he'd cried himself to sleep, his siblings right beside him.

><

"Jon, what do you say you lead us in another round of cheers for Malarya Snark, the hero of Wintersmells?"

"The hero of Wintersmells!" repeated everyone in unison.

"Oh," said Jon from the head of the Great Hall. "Yeah. Proud of you, sis," said Jon wiping his eyes. "Everyone give it up for Malarya."

In response, the crowd in the Great Hall hooped and hollered for thirty straight minutes.

"That was great," said Jon, suddenly snapping out of a thousand-yard stare. "Here's to a great night to celebrate our victory—"

"The hero of Wintersmells!" shouted someone in the crowd.

"Yeah, that's her. Just remember that this was a group effort and that we're having a mass funeral pyre tomorrow to honor all the dead—"

"Malarya J. Snark! The hero of Wintersmells!"

Jon downed several consecutive ales and then pulled Pantsa and Malarya aside as the celebration got going.

"Malarya, it's cool that you killed the Nighty Night King and all, but I guess, well, is it not kind of cooler that I'm the rightful heir to the Pointy Chair?" he said, trying very hard to look casual about it.

"What?" said Pantsa.

"Jon, is this true?" asked Malarya.

"Oh," said Jon, fake laughing, "and I guess I fucked my aunt too? No big deal, haha."

Malarya looked at Jon incredulously. Could he have actually fucked his aunt? If so, that would have been awesome, but he was wasted right now. The odds it was true were slim.

"Here's the thing guys. Keep this on the down low, but dad isn't my dad. His sister is."

"Dad's sister is your dad?"

"*Was* my dad," corrected Jon. "She's dead."

"What?"

Thirty minutes later, Pantsa and Malarya had gotten enough coherent details to understand Jon's lineage.

"That means Dennys is my aunt, and so I fucked my aunt," he said, raising both of his arms for a double high five. "But no, Malarya, it's actually really cute that you killed the Nighty Night King. That's like a good start at doing awesome things," he said, putting his arms down after not getting either high five. "Bottom line is this: Dennys will pretty much do whatever I say. I'm sure I could tell her that I'm gonna be king, and it'll be fine. But keep this between us."

"But Jon, people need to know," said Pantsa. "We have to tell—"

"Ah buh-buh-buh!" said Jon. "We'll talk later. Right now, my people are counting on me to go be the life of this party!" he shouted, before returning to the corner to drink alone.

~⚜~

"Whoremund," said Jon from the floor, much later, as he sobered up in the late hours of the night. "Whoremund."

Whoremund grunted back, lying face down next to Jon.

"You gotta take the Mildlings back north. You gotta take Toast too. Don't try to talk me out of it. You belong up there. This isn't your fight."

Whoremund grunted again.

"Okay, cool," said Jon. "I'm glad you're on board."

"Jon," said Lord Varysectomy, approaching politely. "May I speak to you in private?"

"Anything you have to say in front of me you can say in front of Whoremund. Isn't that right Whoremund?"

Finally Whoremund mustered the strength to roll to face Jon. "Can you *please* shut up?"

"Very well, somewhere private it is," said Jon, leading Varysectomy out to the Carol N. Snark Memorial Coup d'État Planning Courtyard. The stars were brighter than they had ever appeared since Jon's childhood. Perhaps the eradication of the army of the undead had brought some light back to the world. Everything seemed to be on the up-and-up for Westopolis.

"Westopolis is on the down-and-down, Jon," Varysectomy said frantically once he was sure they were alone. "I know you have the rightful claim to the Pointy Chair. You must take it."

"Who told you? Malarya? Pantsa?" Jon's eyes darted around nervously.

"Pantsa told Beerion."

"Damn. And that little snot told you?"

"No, he told a couple of the whores at the brothel."

"Ah, and you went for a visit, to get them to . . . touch your . . . stump? And they told you?"

"No they told Linda Miller, who's a total blabbermouth."

"Aha. Linda. The blabbermouth. A staple of the Wintersmells community indeed. And she blabbed to you."

"No, she kept her mouth shut. But Juan Arenas, do you know him? Good guy. Anyway, he overheard the whores Beerion told while he was getting a suckjob at the brothel from a different whore."

"Those damn whores! Cannot keep their mouths shut!"

"Yes, well, Jon, I suppose that's part of the job description," chirped Varysectomy cheekily.

"Now, *that*. That is a clever double entendre. You can't just shoot a double entendre off like that from the hip," Jon laughed.

"Yes, well, I have little children who write quips for me. I call them birds."

"So this Juan fellow told you?"

"No. Heard it from Lisacious Stoverick. No idea where he heard it from."

"DOES EVERYONE IN THIS GODDAMNED TOWN KNOW ABOUT MY SECRET CLAIM TO THE POINTY CHAIR?!" shouted Jon.

A villager stuck his head out from his frosty window. "Congrats on the claim to the Pointy Chair, Jon!"

Another villager peeped out. "Yeah and huge stuff with the fucking your aunt and everything. That's mad cool!"

"I don't have a claim!" shouted Jon. He stormed off, steaming. "And it is NOT cool to fuck your aunt. Or no, it is cool! But I didn't fuck her! Or wait, no. I DID fuck her, but she is NOT my aunt!"

Lord Varysectomy shook his head. He scuffled along to catch up with Jon. "Listen, I worry about Dennys ruling Westopolis. For all intents and purposes she is an outsider. A refugee from across the ocean for the Gods' sakes. There is only one true, rightful heir to the chair. And it is you, Jon Dough."

"I will never betray my queen."

"Such integrity. Such virtue. But you must realize, Jon...this *will* mean that the whole world will never know that you made love to your aunt..." Varysectomy said coyly.

"I *fucked* my aunt, dammit! Agh! Damn you, eunuch! You will not sow seeds of doubt into my mind!" Jon stormed off again, steaming once more.

"What did I miss?" groaned Squirt Bevlidge, a Snark soldier who'd gotten so blackout drunk during the prebattle festivities that he was only just now waking up on the ground. "Are we going to fight the zombos now?"

"We won," replied Jon as he passed him on the walk to his bedroom. "You can go back to sleep."

"Awww, man!" said Squirt, kicking a helmet on the ground and hurting his toe, but only a little bit.

Lemme

Lemme barged into Brian of Fart's room. He was half in the bag. The other half of him was so drunk that it had long since abandoned the bag and instead proudly displayed his drunkenness. He was fully naked.

"What do you think you're—"

"Shummy shushy shhh shh," said Lemme, slamming into the ground face first without catching himself. "You think I'm sexy, I think I'm sexy, why haven't we fucked yet?"

"Lord Lemme, you're drunk. You don't mean it," Brian said indignantly.

"Well, excuuuuuse me for caring about the environment. *Our* environment, might I remind you! We all have to live in it we might as well take—excuse me," he burped, "take care of it!"

"What in the seven hells are you talking about? You're truly piss drunk!"

Face firmly planted into the cold hard ground and raising his butt to the sky, Lemme began to pee. "The only thing piss about me is...hold on I had something clever for this," Lemme said, confused.

Brian shook her head. Once Lemme had finished relieving himself, he slowly rose to his feet. "Now then," he burped, "let's begin."

"Listen, Lemme," Brian said beginning to warm up ever so slightly. "I cannot lie. I have thought about you once or twice. A day. Every single day. Since I met you. Thought about how much I want to make love to you, that is." Brian began to blush. "But I...I have never been with a man. I am not sure I am ready."

"Perhaps just one kiss, then," Lemme slurred as he wiped some of the dirt from his mouth.

"Well..."

"Hmmm?"

"Well, I suppose just one..."

Lemme gave Brian a peck on the cheek.

"There. I have cum," Lemme said, flopping onto his back and immediately beginning to snore. His pants were soaked with gallons of semen.

At first Brian was shocked. But as she lay down and watched the candlelight flicker on the ceiling, she began to smile. "I am a virgin no longer," she said. Her heart pounding contentedly, she drifted off to blissful sleep.

Dennys

S earching for Jon, who had slipped away from the banquet hall amid the revelry, Dennys poked her head into every bedroom door, trash heap, and laundry chute she could find in the hallways of the fortress. She needed to speak with him earnestly once again about their impending siege of King's Landing Strip and quiet her fears regarding his claim to the Pointy Chair. After an hour, she had walked in on a dozen couples in their bedrooms, her clothes were coated with garbage from the trash piles, and her hair was covered in urine and shit from the laundry chutes.

Eventually, Dennys found a heavy wooden door that opened into a candlelit bedroom where she spotted movement. The hunched figure reeked of whiskey, which reminded Dennys of Jon's cologne, which was a spray bottle full of what Dennys now suspected consisted only of whiskey.

"Are you drunk?" she asked softly.

"Nop," Jon replied. He was drunk. He sat on one side of a chess board, and his hand rested on an intricately carved black mahogany king piece. "I guess nows that Imma king, I can move my pieces in any direction," he slurred thoughtfully, taking burps throughout for dramatic effect. He picked up a pawn and moved it ten spaces sideways. "Chessmate."

Then he shuffled over to the opposite side of the board. "Okay, okay, you win," he said to the empty space where he had just been sitting.

"Are you sure you're not drunk?" asked Dennys, who noticed that Jon had at some point removed both queen pieces from the board and discarded them in a heap in the fireplace.

"I'm not sdjrunk."

Dennys wasn't convinced that he was not sdjrunk. She had been finding it difficult to trust Jon lately, after he had realized he had a legitimate claim to the chair, and also because he had told her that forest fairies didn't exist when Dennys had literally seen one with her own eyes a few years ago. Dennys scratched a straight line into the floorboards with her heel. "If you're sober, can you prove it by walking on this line, one foot after the next, while telling me I'm as sexy as a big white horse with big white horse hooves?"

"You're as sexy as a big white horse."

"With big white horse hooves?"

"Sexier."

Dennys smiled for a moment but quickly returned to her stern demeanor. She held up a finger. "Can you fol-low this finger with your eyes, while standing on one leg, and swearing to never tell anybody about your claim to the throne?"

"What? No."

"Oh my Gods. You're drunk."

Jon saw fear behind Dennys's gleaming violet eyes as she reached out for Jon's cheek and stroked it. He fol-lowed her finger with his eyes, and they rolled up into the back of his head.

"Jon, this truth will destroy us. You cannot tell your sisters who you are. They'll hate me."

"That is impossible, Dennys. How can *my* sisters hate you when, biologically speaking, they don't exist?" He lifted Dennys's face to his. "I'll always be loyal to you. If I were a dog, you'd be a different dog whom I was extremely loyal to. But I cannot keep this a secret."

Dennys's eyes were pleading. "Why not?"

Jon's eyes were still stuck at the top of his head. "Exactly how many kings, do you think, have fucked their aunts?"

Dennys was quiet. "I don't know, Jon. Not many."

"Right. So exactly how fucking *cool* is it, then, that I fucked my aunt?"

"I don't know."

"Fucked my aunt, who probably fucked my uncle, so I basically fucked my uncle too?"

"Jon, don't say that."

"I can't just keep this to myself bwaaaeerrp," said Jon, burping. "I would become such a slegend with the boys in black if they knew. They need to know how we did it doggy style. They need to know how we did it on a boat. They need to be given a recounting, in too much graphic detail, of our sex in full high definition every, say, Sunday night. Not to mention, if everyone knows the Snarks aren't really my sisters, I can finally bang Pantsa!"

Dennys's eyes watered. "Jon, that is disgusting! I am begging you. Do not tell anyone about this."

But Jon's mind was already racing. "Let's hook up again, Dennys. But this time, let's role-play that my parents died and you become my legal guardian, because you're my closest living relative. Oh, wait, I forgot, my parents *are* dead! We don't even have to pretend!" He had never been more turned on in his life.

⪢⪡

The terrifying possibility of Jon's betrayal sat uncomfortably in the back of Dennys's mind as their combined forces prepared to set sail for King's Landing Strip to retake the Pointy Chair. Occasionally, Dennys stopped worrying about Jon and instead thought about how pointy the Pointy Chair really was. If it *was* so pointy, pointy enough to have earned that name, how could anybody sit on it? Was her raid on the Strip worth the puncture wounds? Did Cervix have an especially voluptuous bottom? Probably.

Soon after the ships had pulled away from the bay, the sudden appearance of a fleet bearing Cervix's flags on the horizon brought her mind back to present threats. It was the Ironic Fleet. Dennys, perched on her dragon's back, felt her heart sink as more and more rows of ships approached. Dennys counted them carefully. "One, two, three, four, five, eight, nine, ten, eleven, twelve, eleven, fourteen, fifteen, six, seven, eight, nine, ten, eleven . . ."

"Two hundred ships," shouted a sailor down below.

Two hundred. Whoa. Dennys counted on her fingers carefully to check how many dragons she had left. "One, two."

Two was probably a lot of dragons, she supposed. But the confident faces of the approaching captains filled her with unease. Arrows began to fly, and Dennys's ships were clearly outnumbered. Dennys hopped on Jragon, knowing she'd need to pull out all the stops for this one.

"*Gasolina* times two!" she shouted.

Jragon and Dragun each breathed out beams of fire, then combined their beams together into one megabeam, except that each of their fire beams was a double fire beam as per Dennys's command, making the combined mega-beam a quadruple fire beam. The enemy ships could probably withstand a double beam and maybe even a triple beam. But a quadruple beam? The ships were toast.

One after the other, enemy ships went up in smoke, meaning one after the other, hundreds of children lost their fathers—fathers who nobly put food on the table each night by serving as naval soldiers. Dennys was in the middle of ravishing these fathers and their boats when suddenly Yourmoms Playboy, leading the Ironic Fleet, began calling.

"Hey, dragons! Come to papa! Papa being me, that is," shouted Yourmoms, who stood at the front of his ship with more than sixty men, all gripping the massive sword designed specifically to kill Dennys's dragons. After the last huge sword had failed to kill them, Sideburn rebuilt it, this time out of metal rather than wood, and this time much larger than the original—nearly 1.2 times as big.

Pssh, thought Dennys. *How in the seven hells does he expect to get my dragons to fly near that thing? We're totally safe.*

Yourmoms ripped off a tarp and revealed a mechanism that dangled a horse corpse in front of the giant sword. Except it wasn't just a horse: it was a pony. And not just a pony: it was the pony version of a miniature horse.

Jragon instantly dove straight at the alluringly rare miniature pony corpse.

"Jragon, no!" shouted Dennys. But it was too late. A little ejection pod containing Dennys came shooting out of Jragon's back, landing her safely on the surface of her queen ship. Dennys could only watch as Jragon was completely skewered by the massive blade. In his final movements, he squeaked slowly further down onto the sword and got his tongue just an inch away from the horse-pony-horse corpse. A lucky wind gust brought the delicious corpse to his tongue, and he died happy. The happiest he had ever been.

Yourmoms quickly had his men remove the sword and use it to cut off Jragon's head for good measure. Then they used the giant sword to mince up the rest of his body into bite-sized pieces to be extra safe. Then they used the sword to mince up those pieces into even smaller pieces that were practically liquid just in case. Finally, they checked the liquid's pulse.

Dennys said a bad word under her breath.

"What?" asked the soldier closest to her.

"Oh, sorry." Dennys said the same word again, but louder so that he could hear her. The word was "bollocks."

At the same time, a Funsullied ship was boarded by enemy sailors. They used swords to force the Funsullied into a line on the deck. "Which one of you," cried out the enemy commander, "is Ms. Andei?"

Ms. Andei winced in fear. Who would sell her out? None of the Funsullied spoke. "I'll say this one more time. Which one of you is the woman called Ms. Andei?" More silence. Then a sailor finally spoke. She had lived down the street from Ms. Andei her entire life. "I'm really sorry, I have no idea who that is." Ms. Andei's friends and compatriots nodded in agreement or offered halfhearted shrugs. "If you could describe what she looks like, I'm sure we'd all be happy to help."

Ms. Andei glanced from the spacious escape raft that was being covertly lowered into the water to the

Funsullied soldiers lined up on the middle of the deck. She decided to take the risk. She ran straight to the middle of the line of soldiers. "Are you kidding me?" she screamed at her so-called friends. "You don't know who I am? I'm Ms. Andei. I'm popular, and cool, and relevant, and—" Before she could finish the sentence, hands grabbed her, gagged her, and handcuffed her. Ms. Andei howled in pain as she was taken away.

Content with their prisoner, Cervix's fleet began to recede toward the Strip's harbor. Dennys knew that they expected her to follow, but her hands were tied. She could not let Ms. Andei perish at the hands of Cervix's men. No, no. Far too stinky of hands. Follow she did.

⌦

The silver-haired queen looked up at the golden-haired queen from the foot of the stone wall where Beerion had negotiated a momentary truce. Ms. Andei stood on a precarious platform close to the edge, staring at Dog Shit. A dozen archers watched Cervix, arrows aimed at the Dragon Queen, ready to end the negotiation before it had begun. Cervix held up her right hand, palm open. Beerion knew this could go one of two ways.

Cervix slowly closed her hand into a fist, and Beerion winced. Solemnly, she stuck out her thumb and pinky finger. She rotated her hand from side to side and said to the archers flanking her, "Hang ten, my dudes." Somehow, her lips did not curl into even the slightest of smiles while she said it. The archers obeyed her signal and put away their weapons. Beerion sighed in relief. He approached his sister.

"The Queen in the South, Dennys Grandslam, demands that you surrender." Cervix did not respond. Beerion's voice softened. "Sister, your reign may be over, but think about your baby. Your child—my dear nephew—doesn't have to die this way. There are easier ways to abort him. You could bludgeon your stomach with a veal mallet, or put leeches in your vagina, or do the worm on a bed of nails. Several of my unborn children have gone this way, and I've never heard a single complaint from them *or* their prostitute mothers. Alternatively you could surrender and give birth to this child, I suppose."

Cervix said nothing to her brother. The distance between her advisors and the rebels below the fortress was so great that the half-foot-tall Beerion appeared as only a speck in the dirt. He was frozen with fear as he spoke to the queen, all the while watching Ms. Andei quake while being held by the executioners. After a moment, Cervix realized she was staring at an actual speck of dirt, and her brother had been pounding his belly with a mallet and making whale noises on the ground further in the distance. She had no idea what he was going on about. The golden-haired queen approached Ms. Andei. "If you have any last words, now is the time."

Dennys caught Ms. Andei's gaze and watched in silent horror as Ms. Andei nodded, straightened her body, and triumphantly uttered one word.

"*Gasolimno!*"

Dragun confusedly looked at Dennys. Was Ms. Andei trying to do the dragonfire command? Did she think it was *gasolimno*? Gosh, what a moron.

Dennys's heart sank. That was a message for her. Sort of. She was definitely attempting to say *gasolina*. Right? There would be no peace. Ms. Andei dropped her head solemnly as she realized her queen would not save her in her hour of need. Tears fell from her face as she prepared for the Building to behead her.

Slowly, Sideburn creeped out from behind the legion of Bangsister soldiers perched atop the city wall. He whispered something in Cervix's ear, and after a moment of skeptical contemplation, she motioned for the Building to resheathe his sword. Sideburn walked forward and stared into Ms. Andei's eyes. He cracked all of his knuckles and limbered up before producing a small golden pocket watch.

"You are getting very sleepy, Ms. Andei," he said, dangling the watch in front of her.

Ms. Andei tried to fight the ensuing yawns with all her might but, alas, zonked herself asleep in an instant.

"You see," cackled Sideburn, "I've trained myself in the dark arts of hypnotism, and I have learned all the most sinister savoir faires. Poor Ms. Andei will do anything I tell her in the suggestible state she is now in."

"Wake up!" cried Dennys, but it was too late. Ms. Andei was completely hypnotized.

"Now, Ms. Andei," continued Sideburn, "I want you to dance like a chicken."

"NOOOOOOOOOOO!" cried Dennys. "YOU BASTARD!"

"Bok bok bok!" said Ms. Andei, dancing like an idiotic chicken.

"Heeheehee," cackled Sideburn. "Now cry for your mommy!"

"I want my mommy! Mommy! I need milk!" shouted Ms. Andei, with no regard for how embarrassing this was.

"YOU HAVE DONE ENOUGH! YOU'LL ROT IN THE SEVEN HELLS FOR THIS, SIDEBURN!" Dennys wept inconsolably.

"Now kill yourself!" said Sideburn.

"Dang," said Dennys, as Ms. Andei snapped her own neck off. "That's too bad." Dennys was so broken up about Ms. Andei's death that she declared a one-and-a-half-hour lunch break instead of the normal hour-long one. There would be no peace.

⁓⁕⁓

The tension between the rival queens and the threat of a successful siege loomed over King's Landing Strip more than ever before. Alone in her tent, Dennys was haunted by other thoughts. Betrayal was imminent, she knew. She would need to make difficult decisions in the days to come.

At night, Beerion visited Dennys at the opening to her tent. She had been refusing to eat or sleep since Ms. Andei's death. She only chewed on pieces of expensive salted meats, fishes, fine game hens, oysters, caviar, beef Wellingtons, and chocolates before spitting them out.

And she had developed a voracious cocaine habit in order to prevent herself from sleeping.

Beerion spoke. "There's something you need to know." Dennys didn't turn to face him. She already knew what was coming.

"Panda bears eat up to sixteen hours a day."

"That is correct." Beerion crossed "Tell Dennys About Panda Diets" off the first line of his Best Man To-Do List, then moved to the next item. "Also, Varysectomy is plotting against you. I told him about Jon."

"You what?!"

"That's correct...sixteen hours a day."

Later that night, Dennys summoned Varysectomy to the keep where she chained her dragon. He sank to his knees before her, and she began a speech she had only used a handful of times. "I, Dennys Grandslam, first of her name, Mother of Jon Dough, Fucker of Horses, and Aunt of Dragons, I mean, Aunt of Jon, Mother of Horses, and Fucker of Dragons, hereby sentence you to a fate far worse than death. I sentence you to become a double eunuch."

"Not my butt!" pleaded Lord Varysectomy. "Without my butt I'll be just like one of those Funsullied. Except without the strength. Or discipline. Or fighting prowess. Or cool name."

Dennys lowered Varysectomy's pants. She lifted an enormous sword, carved in iron and encrusted with jewels, and dropped it on her foot because she'd stopped working out ever since she started sleeping with Jon. He did all the

heavy lifting, jar opening, and friendship-bracelet braid-
ing around the castle. So Dennys unsheathed a second,
smaller sword, which she used to remove the packaging
from a third, medium-sized sword. She picked it up and
swung it down onto Lord Varysectomy's backside, slicing
his buttocks cleanly off. Varysectomy, howling in agony
and humiliation, died.

"Damn. A fate worse than death, this was not," sighed
Dennys, glancing down at the floppy, shapeless butt rolling away on the ground.

⇒⋲

There was little time to mourn. The next days were filled
with frantic preparations for the raid on the Strip. Troops
were rallied, horses and prostitutes were mounted, and
black-market organ dealers prepared coolers with ice and
plastered "Semiannual Sale" signs through the streets of
the Strip's neighboring cities.

The first major assault would occur on the sea, with
Dennys's ships bombarding the Ironic Fleet from the sea
and Dragun raining fire down from the sky. Even with
Dragun, the sheer size of the Ironic Fleet meant the battle
would be uphill. Thankfully they didn't encounter any hills
in that area of the ocean. Dragun fought with the strength
of one thousand men plus one slightly smaller dragon. Fire
exploded from the sky, incinerating ship after ship.

Yourmoms unveiled the giant dragon-killing sword
once again, this time with a mostly live human baby dangling in front of it. Dragun flew straight toward the tasty

baby waiting to be devoured. Dennys would have to think fast if she wanted to get out of this situation, leaving both Dragun and the baby unharmed. But Dennys couldn't think that fast. She quickly commanded Dragun to send the baby into flames. Dragun burnt it mostly to a crisp, yet somehow left Yourmoms, who'd been cradling the baby with his arms, completely unharmed. Totally overcooked, the baby was now worthless. This infuriated Dragun. He began demolishing ships out of disappointment.

As the Ironic Fleet began to burn and the crews' spirits began to break, the Ironic soldiers cried out, "Oh, I just LOVE choking on smoke and breathing the smell of my brothers' burning flesh!" "Gee, Dennys, it'd sure be swell if you could just gouge my eyes out and leave me to bleed to death or worse!" "I'm loving this total destruction of my prosperous and exciting life!" "I definitely didn't just pee myself!"

While the last survivors' words bubbled below the surface of the raging sea, the land charge led by the Cloth-khaki and Funsullied began on the Strip. The queen's soldiers fought fiercely until they saw the shadow of Dragun approach from the shore.

～❦～

"Papa, what is that?" asked a frightened teenage boy serving in the Bangsister army. His armor barely fit him at such a young age.

"Oi, innit I tell ya that you would see a real live dragon one day, son? Innit I done do that den?" spoke his father,

221

a senior officer in the army, proud that his promise had finally come true to his boy—his only boy.

"I love you, papa."

"I love you too, son."

"*GASOLINA!*" Dennys unleashed a blood-curdling scream, turning the father-son duo into ash.

"Pa, what is that giant pile of black dust over there?" asked a nearby teenage boy, also serving in the army.

"Roight-o, son. Innit I dun tell ye that yee'd see a two-meter-tall pile a human ash one day son?"

"I can't believe it came true."

"I love you, son."

"I love you, pa. You know, if we were to die right now due to the incinerating flames of some magical beast, well, that would just be alright with me."

Dennys flew right past this father-son duo to demolish more densely populated areas of the city. Most of the city dwellers died of fear, and some of them died of unrelated but conveniently timed natural causes right then and there in the shadow of the dragon.

From the center in the capital, the city bells began to chime to the unmistakable tune of the song "We Surrender" by Ed Sheeran and the Bangsister Boys.

Children choked on smoke, and parents dove to protect them from flames. Popsicles sold by street vendors melted at an alarming rate. Chickens laid eggs, and they immediately turned hard-boiled. Dennys brought Dragun to the ground with an earth-shattering thud.

Coughing and swerving amid the chaos, Beerion ran up to Dennys on his teeny-tiny legs.

"The bells are ringing. The city surrenders. You need to stop the attack."

Dennys made no motion to halt her forces. "I am not stopping until Cervix tells me, face-to-face, that the throne is mine. I am not stopping until all the people of this world are free and all the oppressors face their fate. I don't know how long that will take but probably at least until dinnertime."

Beerion shook his head. "Six o'clock?"

"Seven-thirty."

"Thousands will die in that hour and a half, Dennys. Maybe even billions." He reached to the Best Man of the Queen badge on his cloak. It felt like a lifetime ago that he had designed it himself, back when he'd had hope for the world's uncertain future and this new, mysterious queen. The badge was made of forged metal, and an intricate circular carving portrayed a man in a tuxedo standing next to a woman in a wedding dress. The man wore a ball and chain around his ankle and appeared to be moping, while the woman seemed to be yelling. She had her arms crossed. Beerion didn't know what it meant or where he remembered seeing the symbol, but he had modeled the woman on his badge after Dennys as a tribute.

Beerion ripped it off and threw it down the palace steps, where it skewered an unsuspecting wild rabbit. The rabbit began a short-lived but glorious reign as Best Rabbit of the Queen.

Dennys, accompanied by her whiskered new advisor, turned her attention to leading the army deeper into the city toward the Red Queef. Before they moved on, she laid out her strategy. Beerion had never approved of it. He had called it "completely stupid—you clearly don't understand what a death record means," but Dennys no longer answered to Beerion. She spoke out loud and clear.

"Funsullied, Clothkhaki, rabbit, and spies. I've spent the past months doing research on what the deadliest places in the city are. I have scoured death records and obituaries. I have found that, unequivocally, most people die in orphanages, hospitals, and old folks' homes. This means that they are the most deadly and dangerous places in the city. We will strike these locations first, with no mercy. It's the best way to protect the innocent and vulnerable. Are you with me?"

The army whooped and cheered. Clothkhaki reared up on their horses. Funsullied asked around in confusion, trying to find someone who could translate what their queen had just said. The Dragon Queen marched onward.

Cervix

Cervix Bangsister watched as her city was helplessly ravaged, horrified that she might be next but feeling pretty neutral about the crumbling buildings and dying peasants. *Maybe I'll be fine*, she thought wishfully. *After all, the last time someone penetrated the Red Queef's defenses, it was hundreds of years ago when the city and the kingdom were taken over by the Grandslams with their dragon army—oh, I am absolutely done for.*

Cervix could only watch Dennys fly her dragon over a consecutive row of orphanages, torching them all without hesitation. *No matter how much I hate that Dragon Queen*, thought Cervix, *I can't help but respect the hell out of the choices she makes.*

"Come to mama," she vengefully muttered, before sorrowfully remembering that all her own prepubescent children had passed well before their time. A tear slid down her face—an important sanity check that gravity was working—and a reminder that Cervix never got the chance to teach her children about the simple joys of life: spooning each other, fucking each other, and fucking each other with spoons.

Smoke trailed behind Dragun as he zipped and soared through the sky, leaving a beautiful cursive message for all of the Strip to see: "PREPARE TO BURN: IT'S BURN O'CLOCK." All the townspeople saw the beautiful handwriting, and although they couldn't read, they could still deduce from the massive fires and smoking buildings that it was in fact burn o'clock and that they should prepare.

Cervix observed as Dennys flew to the last standing orphanage in the Strip: Pat's Extra-Broke Orphanage for the Saddest and Most Tragic Kids Who Also Are Bad at Athletics.

"*Gasolina!*" shouted Cervix from her window, trying to beat Dennys to the punch and undermine her ever so slightly. Dragun unleashed an eruption of flames onto the building in the shape of two prospective adoptive parents shaking their heads "no" and walking out of the orphanage in the hopes of finding better kids.

Luckily, when the ornately shaped flames hit, all the children were in the orphanage's kiddie pool and thus were saved from the hellish fires. Unluckily, none of those unathletic kids knew how to swim, so they all drowned, and every single one of them got sent straight to the seven hells because of their lame deaths.

Dennys turned her attention to the Red Queef, locking eyes with Cervix at a distance. They both knew that they were staring at each other, and neither wanted to be the first to blink, but they were both so incredibly far away that it would truly be impossible to tell if either one did. This stalemate between the queens went on for two hours.

Dennys flew to Cervix, hovering as best she could in front of her balcony, which meant she was rising and falling ten to twenty feet in the air every second with the flapping of Dragun's wings. The result of this continuous up-and-down motion was that everything Dennys said to Cervix was constantly fluctuating in both volume and pitch.

"CERvix, it's the END of the LINE," said Dennys as Cervix strained her neck, rapidly looking up and down to follow her. "THE city IS rinGING the bells. THEY SURRender. NOW IT'S time YOU surrenDER! I'VE won."

Cervix knew the Dragon Queen was right, but she didn't want to admit it.

"Fine," said Cervix, knowing she was out of options. "I slur blenders."

"What?" shouted Dennys, landing on the balcony. "You have to say the actual words. Say you surrender." To prove that she would accept nothing but the correct verbiage, Dennys unleashed another devastating stream of fire from Dragun upon the city.

"I did," said Cervix, darting her eyes around. "I stir tenders."

"You can't just say stuff that sounds like 'surrender.' That's not a loophole that stops you from having to surrender."

"What loophole?" asked Cervix, unconvincingly pretending like that wasn't her plan. "I told you already: I blur gender!"

Dragun burned down another section of the Strip.

"Fine! Yes! I was trying to use a loophole. I spur vendors! Happy?"

Another five neighborhoods set ablaze.

"Say it. Say 'I surrender.'"

"You surrender?" asked Cervix, feeling very smart. "Well, if you insist!"

"Okay, no," said Dennys. "Stop trying these little tricks. I have a dragon and burned your entire city down. This is purely symbolic."

"Ugghhh," moaned Cervix. She knew Dennys had won. "I don't even care! I surrender. I never wanted to be queen anyway. This city sucks ass, and Westopolis is horseshit. The Pointy Chair isn't fun to sit in. Now put your dragon to rest."

A dark, menacing smirk came across Dennys's face. "Very good. That wasn't so hard, was it? Well, I'm off to continue melting the city," announced Dennys.

"No! You promised! What point is there in further destroying a city that's now your own?!" pleaded Cervix.

"Sorry, dear, but promises are like similes. They don't always hold." Dennys then whispered to herself, "Come to think of it, why should I continue burning the Strip?" She pondered for a moment. "I'm not a quitter? Yeah, sure. I'm Dennys Grandslam, and I never quit!" Dennys mounted Dragun and took off into the sky, this time as queen.

All the hate and pride in Cervix's life began to transform toward the one goal of making it out of this situation alive. And then her goal of making it out of this situation alive began to transform into the goal of having sex with her brother one last time. Cervix ran to give the Pointy Chair one last kiss before leaving to find Lemme. To spite Dennys, she also decided to lick the chair. Immediately Cervix cut her tongue on the swords but kept licking and cutting her tongue until every inch of the chair was covered in her saliva and every inch of her tongue was covered in stab wounds. Cervix crouched down and carved her initials into the bottom of the chair, right under the heart that said "Ser Wensley + Jenny the Prostitute Forever" and just next to the "Winter Sucks!" carving and just above the carving of a busty she-dragon.

As Dennys continued her rampage and Cervix began her descent of the Red Queef's massive staircase, Lemme found his way inside through a second hole entrance at the bottom of the palace. He lusted after Cervix, making his way deeper and deeper into the bowels of his former home. Smoke and dust from the crumbling building obscured his vision, as did the fact that his eyes and whole head were made of solid gold. To navigate, Lemme figured out that he could continually slap himself in the face, making a nice ringy-dingy noise against the metal to echolocate throughout the premises.

But such smacking attracted none other than Your-moms Playboy, who had washed ashore when Dennys's army defeated him and the Ironic Fleet. If Yourmoms was going to die, he was going to bully Lemme one last time and get in some final taunts and barbs.

"Oy there, Goldilocks, you wanna piece of me?" shouted Yourmoms, as he cut off his own ear and threw it at Lemme. *Clang!* It hit Lemme's shiny metal head.

"What? Who goes there!" Lemme greatly increased the frequency of his head smacking to improve his echo-locating capabilities.

"I said.... OY THERE, Goldilocks, you wanna PIECE of ME?!" Yourmoms doubled down, cutting off *another* one of his ears, becoming mostly deaf in the pro-cess. *CLANG!* He chucked it at Lemme; it hit him smack in the temple and let out the perfect ring. With that, Lemme was able to get a picture-perfect echolocated snapshot of his surroundings for a brief second.

And that was all he needed.

Lemme stabbed himself with a dagger and started squirting out a giant pool of blood, which he pushed Yourmoms into. It was gross. It was sticky. And it had Hep C. Yourmoms kept slipping and sliding around in the blood like a fool, humiliated.

Yourmoms used the stream of blood to slip 'n' slide down the corridors of the Red Queef at breakneck speed, breaking his neck in the process.

"Try and catch me now, pretty boy!" shouted Yourmoms. He zipped and zoomed around crumbling corridors like a bloody penguin, somehow still alive. Thinking quickly, Lemme painted a realistic-looking tunnel to outside onto one of the walls of the palace. Yourmoms promptly slid himself into it headfirst. His thick skull smashed through dozens of meters of bricks, causing further structural instability to the already crumbling palace. He was dazed, but he wouldn't give up on getting some great last insults in on Lemme. Using a dull brick, Yourmoms carved a slit down the side of his thigh and removed his femur with his bare hands.

"Look!" shouted Yourmoms, sloppily throwing his femur at Lemme. "Now I can say I've boned Cervix *and* Lemme Bangsister!"

"Oof," groaned Lemme. "That was really bad."

"Yeah, Goldilocks, I made sweet, sugary love to your Bangsister sister. I poured syrup all over our bodies, and then we feasted on the pancake of the flesh." Yourmoms said all of this standing on the last leg of his life, tibia in hand.

Lemme knew what he said must be true. Cervix was a sucker for all things sweet—and umami. He had to win this battle, for love.

"Oh yeah? Well I took her to Philadelphia on vacation and got a honeymoon suite. You wanna know why?" asked Lemme.

Lemme got in real close, all up in Yourmoms's stuff, and with 0.01 decibels said, "Because it's the city of BROTHERLY fucking LOVE."

"The only reason your moldy face can get a room with her is because you shared a womb with her. She wants a man like me, one with guts." Yourmoms lifted his shirt and began cutting open his stomach to reveal his innards.

"Oof, your guts smell really bad, man."

"Oh yeah?" shouted a dizzy Yourmoms, barely able to stand. "Well...my penis is uh, big! Bigger than yours!" he said, going for the cheap shot and miraculously making out words as his ear holes dumped out blood.

"What? That's not even a joke."

"Hm...um, okay. I had uh, um, I *fucked* your sister!" shouted Yourmoms as if he had just said something very clever.

"Yeah, I know. None of these are good burns."

"You uh, um, okay, I got this...YOU had sex with your sister?"

"You're just saying facts."

"My uh, oh this is good, hmm, yes, oh okay. MY HEAD, hurts?"

Lemme had heard enough. He smashed his head into Yourmoms's. Yourmoms let out a blood-curdling scream as he fell to the ground, suddenly realizing that because he'd had sex with Cervix and Lemme had also had sex with Cervix, then by the transitive property, they'd had sex with each other. Yourmoms thought he was way out of Lemme's league.

Smashing his golden head into Yourmoms had given Lemme a perfect gong-like noise with which he was able to echolocate through the entire Red Queef. Through all the walls, halls, and chambers, Lemme was able to get a perfect position on Cervix. Latitude: 50.618952°, Longitude: 165.986255°, forty-four feet above sea level.

Lemme gave a final glance at his mangled rival and spoke words that would echo throughout the course of humankind: "I'm gonna go do incest with my sister."

Lemme sprinted out the door as Yourmoms, on the verge of death, screamed the last insult he'd ever utter.

"Ummm, I…uhhh, you're a big fat—no, wait, okay, you're sooo—no that doesn't make sense, hmm, wait," said Yourmoms. And then Yourmoms closed his eyes forever. Minutes later, he had it: "You *are* a big fat." He died content.

Lemme navigated the halls of the Red Queef, screaming for Cervix.

Cervix reached the bottom of the massive spiral staircase, distraught. She always thought there were 1,890 steps, but there were…1,892?

As she began to climb back up the stairs for a recount, Lemme called out.

"Cervix!"

She turned around to see a battered form of the man she had always loved.

"Lemme?" her eyes filled with tears, mostly because of the dust in the wake of the building collapsing.

The two siblings embraced, holding each other as the Red Queef continued to collapse. Bricks, anvils, and pianos fell from what felt like the sky but was actually the brick, anvil, piano, and banana peel storage room collapsing one floor above them.

A doorway to the wide-open courtyard where they'd be safe from the building collapse was mere feet away. Both Bangsisters wanted to run through it, but neither wanted to ruin the moment, so they stood still and kept making out.

Cervix leaned in to give her war-torn brother a final, parting kiss.

"Until we meet again, death makes us all into children once more," muttered Cervix, as she closed her eyes for the big finale.

Lemme moved his head in way too fast, knocking Cervix hard on the noggin and chipping a few of her teeth.

"Ah! Sorry," he said.

With a toothy smile, Cervix tried again: "And now, with this kiss, my beauty will sleep forever."

Cervix took the lead this time, leaning in to suck her brother's big, shiny metal face.

ZAP! A huge arc of electric current shot from Lemme's lips to Cervix's. All that running around with Yourmoms had built up a formidable amount of static electricity.

More pianos and anvils fell from the upper levels of the Red Queef, trapping the lovers inside a stony, musical tomb. Cervix was fried but gave it one more go.

"Our...our love is like a zoo: enclosed, animalistic, fucked up. Now, kiss me."

Lemme leaned in. This time nothing could interrupt them. They both gave each other a mediocre last kiss with way too much tongue.

And with that, the Red Queef let out its final sigh, collapsing fully to the ground, delighting the Bangsisters with the shared smooch of death.

Beerion

Beerion drunkenly stumbled through the Strip as the city came crumbling down on top of him. His plan was simple: get to the tavern and jump inside a glass of ale. *Dragonfire can't burn me if I'm swimming in a glass of ale*, he thought. *I'll be safe inside the beer. And more importantly, I'll be drunk. Wait a second...* Beerion earnestly checked his face and then down his body with both hands. *I am drunk! Good, good.*

Beerion scurried around the corner, and at last he saw it in all its smelly glory: the tavern, Ye New Taverne. Safety and alcohol were in reach. But before he could get there, something caught his attention. *Holy shit*, thought Beerion, as he watched dozens of naked whores panically sprint through the street. *The brothel must have fallen*. Beerion wiped a tear from his eye. *The city is truly lost.*

But then, something more important caught Beerion's eye. Lengths above, on a tenth-floor balcony of the Red Queef, directly across the street from the tavern where Beerion hid, two freakishly large men were fighting each other. *The Freakishly Large Fighting Men wing of the brothel must've fallen too*, Beerion thought dismally. *Unless…it's only the Clown and the Building?*

The Clown shoved his sword through his brother's chest. "That's for not letting me play with your toy when we were kids!" Then he shoved a dagger through the Building's head. "And that's for burning my face in a fire when I played with it anyway!" Then he shoved a third dagger into his stomach. "And *that's* as much as we know about our character arcs!"

The Building calmly removed all three blades from his body, unaffected. "You mean *this* toy?" he shouted, reaching into his armor and pulling out a jack-in-the-box. He began to furiously wind it while holding it as high up above his head as he could.

"Quit it!" said the Clown, hopping up and down and flailing his arms as the toy's music taunted his ears. "I want a turn! I deserve a turn!" The Clown jumped higher and higher, but he couldn't reach the toy. "Eh, eh, eh," he whined as he jumped. "Come! On!" He couldn't do it. The music from the toy suddenly halted as the jack popped out of the box. The Clown pounded his fists on the ground. "This is not fair!"

"Haw! Haw! Haw!" snickered the Building in his low evil laugh as he began to pet the toy. "What a lovely toy it is that I have to myself."

The Clown began to turn red as his body filled with rage. He couldn't take this much longer.

"Oh yes, it is so sweet to have my special box in which Jack is inside," said the Building. "Such a wonderful bliss I receive when he surprises me by popping out into our world."

That was all the Clown could stand of this torture. He stood up and began to speak. "It's...my... TURRRRRRRRRRNNNNNN!!!!!!!" The Clown took off at full speed, charging at his brother. When the Clown's body made contact with the Building's, he was going so fast and with such passion that it sent them both flying over the balcony while wrapped in each other's arms. The two behemoths fell identically to how Voldemort and Harry fell in each other's arms in the nearly exactly parallel yet legally distinct scene from *Deathly Hallows Part 2*. I, George R. R. Martin, have never seen that movie of course, and I also had the idea first.

Oh shit shit shit, thought Beerion. *Not the tavern. Not the tavern! Land anywhere but the tavern.* Their trajectory was forming a perfect arc toward the tavern just in front of Beerion.

As they soared further and further downward, the two juggernauts of men continued to get hits in on each other for the last time ever.

"No choking!" shouted the Clown. "No choking! I'm telling mom!" He kicked his brother in the nuts.

"Owwwww! Off limits! No balls!" said the Building, pulling the Clown's hair.

"Hair puller! Hair puller!"

"Nut kicker! Nut kicker!"

"I hate you I hate you I hate you I hate you!" they shouted in unison, as their combined eight hundred pounds of body mass fell closer and closer to the load-bearing roof of the tavern until—*CRASH!*—it was over.

~✼~

Beerion couldn't believe his eyes. There on the ground in front of him—right out of the sky—had fallen an unopened six pack. *The Gods are good*, he slurred in his head. Beerion set to work devouring the cans—beer and all. It wasn't until the fifth can of beer that he realized he wasn't getting any drunker. *O'Doulio's Non-Alcoholic Beer?! This can't be. No. No. No.* Beerion panicked as his vision started clearing up and his judgment became sound again. He hadn't had a real drink in minutes, and if he didn't find one soon, his BAC might drop dangerously below seven.

Desperate, Beerion started digging around in the ruins of the Strip. For a while all he could find was mountains of gold jewelry and gemstones, all of which he kicked to the side since he wasn't a little girl. Eventually he unearthed a small flask, but when he opened it he found it only contained water from the Fountain of Youth—not even a single drop of Fireball. He threw it over his shoulder and cursed. For the first time in years, he felt like he could spell his own name. This made him curse harder and more coherently than ever. He kicked the biggest stone that his six-inch frame allowed him to—and underneath that pebble he found a person.

"Finally! Help has arrived!" shouted the man who was buried beneath the pebble.

Beerion was confused. He was sure he knew that voice, but he had no idea from where. He gave up on trying to recognize the man's face, as it appeared to be sliced in half vertically. "Who are you? Do I know you from a tavern somewhere?"

"Oh, m'lord, I know many people across Westopolis. Why, I was just completing a tour of the continent when I ran into this girl up north who..."

The man droned on, and Beerion eagerly awaited the part of his story where he would reveal that he was the owner of the biggest tavern in Westopolis and that he had hidden away hundreds of casks of wine in the little spaces in his body where he'd been split in half, just waiting to be given to the man who dug him up from the rubble.

"...and then I managed to crawl down to the Strip, but just as I made it to the hospital it exploded in front of me! Oh, m'lord, I thought I was going to die under all that rubble. Jolly good of you to rescue me and all—"

As the cold winds of sobriety blew away the last sweet clouds of Beerion's drunkenness, he suddenly remembered who this guy was. "Oh. It's just you. Ed Sheeran." Disappointed, Beerion tossed the pebble back on top of Ed, killing him instantly.

Beerion moved on to another pile of rubble, hoping he'd have better luck there. He moved a large stone and unearthed a young boy whose face he thought he recognized.

"Hallelujah! I'm saved!" yelled the boy, who had a small slice across his throat and was covered in non-life-threatening cuts. "Thank goodness, now I can go back to looking for my family—"

"Spare me the story and just tell me your name," said Beerion, rubbing his eyes as he adjusted to not seeing double.

"My name's Rickety—Rickety Snark. I'm one of the Snarks of Wintersmells—"

Beerion lost interest. Not only did this kid definitely not have alcohol, but he couldn't even bother to come up with the name of one of the actual Snarks. Beerion tossed the stone back on top of the lying boy, as well as a few more stones when the first failed to kill him. As Beerion was walking away, he was hit by a realization. "Wait a minute—'Rickety Snark'..." Beerion turned back to the pile of rocks. "That boy...had the *dumbest* fake name I've ever heard!" Beerion started laughing. He laughed harder than he had in years. He fell to the ground and rolled around, flailing his little arms and kicking his little feet. He laughed so hard he got light-headed and started seeing stars. He was loving this. He almost felt drunk again.

As he rolled around, Beerion kicked his leg into another pile of rubble. He heard a loud *pang* and felt a sharp pain shoot up his leg. He got up and inspected the rubble more closely, shifting aside a few more rocks. He saw a large head made of gold. Beerion moved aside the rest of the rocks and unearthed the body attached to the head, as well as another body.

"Brother...sister..." said Beerion as he furiously patted down the corpses for liquor. The bodies of his siblings lay broken, crushed by the rubble of the Red Queef. The time had finally come: Beerion was the last of the Bangsisters. His brother and sister were his family's last hope for a healthy bloodline to live on. Now they were dead, and their family name would go with them, vanishing into obscurity, their legacy in the new world reduced to nothing more than ink in a history book on some future maester's shelf. And, worst of all, Beerion couldn't find any alcohol on them.

Beerion gave the bodies one last look. Cervix looked peaceful, more kind and queenly than she had ever appeared in life, and Lemme was positioned so that he was sixty-nine-ing her while jerking off and shoving a fist into his prostate.

Beerion fell to the ground, defeated. He began to come to terms with the fact that here, in this crumbling city, he would in all likelihood die. A dirty, sober, six-inch, family-less loser. However, after a moment a smile crept back onto his face when he thought about the name Rickety again.

Jon

B lood, gristle, vomit, scratches, and dents covered Jon's warranty-voided armor as he stood look-ing across the devastation all around him. Before today, the square he stood in had been a bustling center of trade. Now it was a ravaged wasteland.

"Well, I suppose that's just capitalism, eh?" he quipped to himself, unaware of how poignant, yet misplaced, his words were. Bodies lay strewn across the cobblestones; men, women, children, tweens, seniors, and the middle-aged all lay as equals in death. Across the plaza, an army was slowly gathering at the base of the enormous marble steps leading up to the ravaged Red Queef. They gath-ered, gazing up at a lone figure standing at the top of the steps, stark against the blue sky. As he slowly made his way, weaving through the remains of the capital, he could hear snippets of the speech this mysterious figure was giving to the gathered soldiers.

"We will move the prison for the criminally insane across the street from the school for the intellectually gifted and frail."

Who was this mystery woman? Jon had to find out, but that could wait for now. Jon was still a little shaky from the battle, which had been hard fought. The Golden Company, bought with gold, had proved their merit and bravery in the streets and households, on the walls of the city, and in the savage fighting in the sewers. They had paid in blood. And they were obliterated by a single dragon. But theirs wasn't the only sacrifice. Jon himself had taken a heavy blow to the head while headbutting a Bangsister squire to death. A dull roar filled his ears; he would probably never regain the ability to wiggle his ears. And at least temporarily, his eyesight was damaged.

"We will advertise a day at the zoo where paraplegic children get in free . . . oops, we left the tiger exhibit open, and all the kids are covered in BBQ sauce."

The crowd seemed to breathe around him, each individual expanding and contracting like so many pulmonary arteries. But where was Dennys? He could barely make out the orating figure, but he was certain it could not possibly be her. This mystery figure was speaking like a crazy person. And Dennys was not crazy. Surely her burning of the entire city, including the innocent civilians, the children, and the elderly, was a mistake. A joke, maybe. Perhaps just a misunderstanding at worst. Jon's cloudy eyes scanned the city, hoping to see his queen somewhere and console her in the wake of all this unintentional chaos.

"We will destroy the moon, and our Clothkhaki riders will make their advance on the sun and any remaining planets."

This woman, though her speech inspiring, was mad! Bent on nothing but bloodlust! He needed to find Dennys quickly and put a stop to the mysterious figure's insanity. Grunting with effort, Jon overturned a broken piece of stone facade.

"Dennnys? Dennnny, where are you?" Jon called, expecting to see Dennys cowering under the rubble.

"I will now rank the animal crackers by shape. First is the giraffe shape of course... Now the next one is tough because I like the way that I can bite the ears off the lion and it looks like..."

Jon's terror grew by the second. She could be anywhere in the crowd—somebody must have seen her. He ran up the great marble steps, spun to face the crowd, and cupped his hands to amplify his voice.

"Dennnnys? Deeeeennys?" he yelled. The voice of the speaking figure paused, and with it the crowd grew silent. Jon took the chance to address the gathered soldiers. "My name is Jon Dough of House Snark—well, it was, until recently I found out that my father was actually my mother and that my mother was Eggie Grandslam, giving me a rightful claim to the Pointy Chair. I'm looking for Dennys, Collector of Trains, Fan of David Blaine,

Queen of the Sandals, and so on—please, someone, anyone, can anyone tell me where to find her?"

The Funsullied stared sheepishly at the ground. Jon's
eyesight was slowly returning to him. He looked to
Dog Shit, who was awkwardly twirling his foot on the
ground and darting his eyes behind Jon toward the mystery speaker. Jon twirled around, making his way up the
final few steps. This woman, she must know where to
find Dennys. His eyesight improved a little more. As Jon
climbed the last few steps, just at her feet, the mysterious
figure raised her arms in a triumphant *V* and let out a
deep bellow.

*"And then, I'm going to tabletop a bunch of old people,
have a friend get on their knees behind them, and I'll push
them over. Take that, Granny. Boom, good night, Grandpa."*

"Oh, holy hells," Jon sighed. "It is you?" Jon saw her,
his Dennys, standing at the top of the steps, just feet
above him. The massed army clambered behind him in
response to Dennys's emphatic call for bloodshed, but
Jon only had words for his queen. "What are they cheering about?" he asked, his eyebrows arching quizzically.
"We've got a real situation here. I am bound by honor
and duty to tell you to stop all this bloodshed. Please
make sure you don't rile the army up with a rousing call
for violence." The army's swords raised in a cacophonous
rattle. Even the weapons of all the child soldiers could be
heard being dragged on cobblestone.

Dennys stood poised brilliantly above her army of
lovable pickpocketing cockney street urchins, dirty

horse-worshipping warriors, pedophiles, and buttless mercenaries, paying Jon's words no mind. Jon felt his heart sinking deeper and deeper into his chest, his lips forming a puckered *O*. This was not the Dennys he had fallen in love with: the ditzy, free-spirited, cute Dennys. This was a new powerful, strong-willed, independent Dennys. He was appalled by these adjectives. She used to be obsessed with silly, girly things, like freeing all the slaves in the world and treating people well. Now she wanted power and obedience from her followers? What had changed her demeanor?

"I feel like sleeping. I bumped my head earlier. Wow, I'm dizzy," she said as her pupils began to veer in opposite directions. It was clear to anyone with medical training that Dennys had sustained a serious concussion. However, she had been so needed in battle that doctors had gone against their better judgment and declared her fit to play. If exposed to more head injuries, she would surely develop CGE, a Crazy Grandslam Episode. Dennys motioned for Jon to follow her as she turned from her army. Jon jogged to catch up.

As Jon and Dennys receded into the Red Queef, the closing band started to set up their gear.

"Check, mic check."

Funky bass riffs filled the streets of King's Landing Strip. Then the drums kicked in, in a big way. The army started grooving and really feeling themselves. Jon motioned to Dennys that he wanted to hang back and see the band's set.

"Jon, there is no cause to party right now. I have much to do. Much *more* to conquer. Many more flames to unleash on the unsuspecting. Let's talk, in the Pointy Chair room." Dennys motioned toward the ruined Bang-sister hold.

Jon's eyesight finally returned to full strength. "Okay. So it definitely is you." His hearing, however, had not. "And sure, sure, a costume party. The Pointy Chair broom, whatever that is . . . But we really need to talk at some point about what happened today." Lines of concentration appeared around Jon's mouth.

Ash fell like snow as they walked hand in hand toward the Pointy Chair. Jon's tongue was outstretched, trying to catch individual flakes.

"I thought you said we were going to a costume party." Much to Jon's chagrin, he realized he was the only person there who had gone to any sort of trouble to be on theme. "Listen, Dennys, I have to tell you something. Ever since you killed all those poor townspeople with your fire-breathing monster, even though you completely—and let me reiterate with more disgust—*completely* did not have to, I've just . . . I don't think you're such a good person anymore." Jon flinched, expecting to be set aflame immediately.

"Jon," Dennys replied, smiling, "I am still the same Dennys you fell in love with. The same one you fought beside, believed in when times got tough, and the same one you made love to."

"Yeah, I guess we did totally bang," said Jon, wiping away a tear. "Also, I'm over here, Dennys. You've been talking to that plant."

"Sorry. Sorry. I'm just still so dizzy. That bump really did a number on my head. Anyway, that's right. You fucked your aunt, buddy. And more importantly than that, I love you. We can still do this together. We can conquer the world!"

"You're still not quite looking at me. That's the same plant, but I suppose—Dennys, no! No! What am I saying?! You killed all those innocent people! Seven hells, you destroyed the city you wish to rule! You've removed a tyrant, yet in the course became one yourself!"

"Ahem, excuse me." Both Jon and Dennys spun to face the voice. It belonged to a newcomer who had silently slipped into the hall.

"I think I'm lost . . . is the costume party down the hall to the left or right?" Standing where the great oak doors had once held silent guard over the hall was Piffley, Dennys's old flower picker.

"Not now, Piffley," Jon said solemnly, though silently happy that he was not alone in costume. "Keep the costume on. We'll meet up later." Jon's stern demeanor quickly returned to him after a brief moment of imagining all the fun Piffley and he would soon have.

Dennys noticed Jon's anger had returned. She took a deep breath, then addressed Jon directly.

"Jon, I know that you brought me here to question my actions today. I did what needed to be done. I realized what

I had to do to break the wheel. I had an epiphany, the logic of which I can explain to you with metaphors like *a phoenix rising from the ashes*, or *the purative effects of fire*, or *a clean slate*. Stop me when one of these connects, Jon. *Stop the motor of the world*, or *creative destruction*, and then I'll craft *one ring to rule them all*. No wait, that's something else…"

Jon looked out into space, realizing Dennys was far beyond saving. She'd gone mad with power, just as Cervix before her, Robot Boaratheon before her, and the Rad King before him. He kneeled down and cudgeled his brain, trying desperately to formulate some solution that would remove Dennys from power without bringing her any harm. While he contemplated, Dennys continued to ramble on about her manifest destiny, the Clothkhakis' living space, and the like.

Jon realized the only right thing to do was what he should have done hours ago. He'd have to kill Dennys. If she were left alive, tens of thousands more innocent people would die under her reign just as they had today in the Strip. Jon couldn't bear to imagine all those innocent buildings that would still be standing if he'd thought to do this even just a couple hours earlier.

Suddenly Jon hatched a plan. He'd have to catch Dennys off guard to kill her. Jon always kept a blade in the crotch of his pants for personal reasons. He shook his head in disbelief at what he was about to attempt. But it was the best idea he had.

"Yes, uh-huh, that's a very interesting thing you are saying—hey, Dennys," Jon said nervously. "How about, uh, would you wanna give me one last blowjob for old times' sake?"

"*Last* blowjob?" said Dennys, taken aback.

"Uhhh, no! I mean, um, just one more blowjob…of many future blowjobs to come…for old times' sake?"

"Hmmm." Dennys squinted her eyes. Jon did his best not to appear suspicious and violently jerked his head toward his crotch, subtly insinuating his desire once again. "Hmmm," Dennys said again.

Dennys got on her knees as Jon stood getting ready to swing the knife and cut her throat. But then, Dennys began to rub his penis before undoing his pants.

Suddenly Jon experienced a very rational revelation. *Damn*, thought Jon. *This feels really, really good. How can I kill someone who makes me feel this good? Because I can't, that's how. I simply cannot kill my beloved Dennys.*

"You know," said Dennys, "when we do this, I must say, I really appreciate that it's so small."

What? thought Jon. *What the fuck? It is my sworn duty to kill her for the good of the country.*

Dennys undid Jon's pants and saw the knife.

"Hey!" she said. "It's that knife you always keep in your pants for personal reasons."

"But *this* time—*it's* nothing *personal*," quipped Jon slyly, swinging his pelvis left and right until the blade had sliced Dennys's throat open. He hoped somebody had written that one down.

"Listen, kid," Jon said as Dennys bled out on the floor. He lit a cigarette and gestured to her with it. "I liked you, I really did. But sometimes it doesn't matter how much you like someone." Jon put on a pair of period-accurate sunglasses. "You just gotta kill them, and that's the honest to Gods truth, see. And that's just business right there. That's showbiz, Dennys. That's politics."

Dennys grabbed the knife from the floor and cut her throat all the way so she wouldn't have to keep listening to Jon's monologue.

"You hear me, Dennys?" asked Jon. "That's Vegas for you. Texas hold 'em rules. Gotta know when to fold 'em. Dennys? Dennys?" The queen was dead.

Just then, an exasperated squire ran into the room. "Am I too late?" he panted. "I'm here with the Dying Desire Foundation. Sorry, you would not believe how many dying people are out in the streets right now. If I didn't know any better, I'd say a dragon burned them all half to a crisp!"

As the words came out of the squire's mouth, Dragun landed directly behind him in a thunderous thud. The squire froze. Dragun approached his mother's body on the ground. Dragun nuzzled her body, trying to get a reaction. Nothing. He tried again, shoving her body, begging his mom to wake up and give him just a single breath to prove she was alive. Nothing. He tried again, really not accepting that his mom was dead. His efforts became more and more pathetic. Finally he nudged her so hard that her arm snapped off and she failed to react at all. Maybe one more nudge ought to do the trick? But it was no use. His mother was dead. Dragun roared at the top of his lungs in Jon's face, while halfheartedly continuing to nudge Dennys with his talon. He could tell Jon had done this to her.

This is the end, thought Jon as Dragun moved his massive jaws closer to his head. *This beast is going to eat me alive.*

"Ehem," spoke Dragun in an eloquent voice. "How much blood was spilled on this day? How many more parents will bury their children? How many more lives will perish before you stupid men realize that power does nothing but corrupt? I've sat here silently at my mother's helm for years, and all I hear about is this infernal chair. And how small you, Jon Dough, are in bed."

I'm going to have to kill this dragon, thought Jon, darting his eyes toward the snickering squire.

"But no more! Not one more life lost in service of this chair. Today is the day this chair, and all it stands for, comes to an end!" Dragun lifted his head backward and paused for a moment. All was silent in the Red Queef, save for a bellowing echo coming from deep inside Dragun's belly. He lashed his head forward and unleashed the hottest fire he'd ever summoned.

"Aghhh! Ow! Ow OW HOT HOT OWW! Stop!" cried the squire, who was standing directly between Dragun and the chair. "You just said no more lives would be lost because of this chair! You are contradicting—oh my

253

god PLEASE stop—yourself! IT BURNS! Why won't this fire just kill me already? It's melting a literal iron chair behind me!" And just like that, the squire died fifteen minutes later.

The Pointy Chair was melted into a puddle of iron on the floor. It was no more.

After several beats, Dragun picked up Dennys's body and exited through the ceiling, passing out into the ink-blue night. The currents of air in the room began to calm.

Jon lost sight of Dragun in the darkness, until his outlined figure passed in front of the brilliantly full moon. It was clear that Dragun had gripped the fallen queen pretty tightly between his claws; Dennys's body looked like when a water balloon is squeezed in the middle.

"Gross," Jon whispered, wiping a final tear from his face. In the falling silence, he turned and noticed a young fancy lad entering the hall.

"I would be remiss if I didn't honor our fallen leader with a song," announced the lad.

> *"In the grand haaaallll,*
> *we saw our queeen fall,*
> *at the hand of Jon the Small,*
> *his penis, like that of a doll.*
> *Tiny little pecker,*
> *With his knife he did wreck her.*
> *Then the beast spake eloquently.*
> *A squire did he bake relatively.*

The chair has been liquified.
I work almost entirely on tips."

The singing lad now held his hat out to collect tips. Jon tried to avoid eye contact and solemnly walked out of the hall.

Beerion

After weeks of epic journeys from the farthest reaches of the Seven Kingdoms, across the treacherous forests of the East, and through the infamous Westopolis Valleys of Endless Adventure and Infinite Storylines, all the most powerful lords and ladies finally arrived at King's Landing Strip. Yes, journeys so incredibly arduous and intriguing, their stories could surely fill another two, perhaps three, novels. Yet, for the sake of the leather on my publisher's whip, I will summarize all of their journeys with a single anecdote: Whoremund looked at a rock. *Rock*, thought Whoremund.

Westopolis's best were in attendance at King's Landing Strip, sucked in from their various homes by the vacuum of power created by Queen Dennys's death. They sat in silence on stools arranged in a half circle outside the rubble of the Red Queef. They sat arranged according to the following logic:

All of the Snark children sat together, arranged in either ascending or descending height. The only people sitting closer to the rightmost edge of the half circle than Ser Boats McSeaman had to have more vowels in their name than him. Whoremund sat next to two people he had never met before, unless he sat next to Bland, in which case he'd know the person on the other side of him as well. Ham sat on the leftmost end of the semicircle, with no more than two women sitting an odd number of people away from him. No seat was left empty, unless someone had designated it empty so they could prop their legs on it, but they were only allowed to do so if they had showed up to the meeting fifteen minutes early. Using this information you can deduce the order. I suggest you use no more than five minutes on this problem as the rest of the book will be worth more points.

There was a solemn feeling of uncertainty in the air. Everyone was on eggshells. There were eggs all over the fucking ground. "The ground that I *just* swept," said Mortimer, the late queen's personal janitor, as he continued sweeping up mountains of rubble. Mortimer was a true gift to the royal family; a rare reminder of integrity in the cold world of Westopolis, he remained loyal to the Bangsisters even after his queen's death. A veritable gem among the filth and deceit commonplace in King's Landing Strip. Perhaps he would not be confined to remaining a janitor his whole life... Perhaps there was more in store for him. Much more.

Dog Shit arrived and stabbed Mortimer in the heart. "Hello," he said to the lords and ladies sitting in the semicircle. He held onto a chain, which held Beerion's tied hands at the end.

"You know, Dog Shit," began Pantsa Snark, "you mustn't kill someone every time you make an introduction. You can just say hello."

"No, I may not. For I am a Funsullied. And that means that I have no butthole."

"Right, but, well... that isn't logical at all."

"My lady," Dog Shit drifted off, looking up to the sun with a fierce squint and then returning his glance to lock eyes with Pantsa. He began, "You see, long ago, a man removed my butthole, and from that day I was a Funsullied. Day and night I would train with the most vicious, powerful men our master could find to pit me against. And I did it all without a butthole. I would eat, sleep, and breathe Funsullied; yet deep down I wanted a different life. But, without a butthole, even if I managed to escape my master, nobody would take me seriously. My only hope was to meet a sorcerer and pay them a substantial sum of money. Enough money for them to perform ancient blood magic upon me, reinstating my butt. I have long searched for a sorcerer. Everyone I see, I sometimes think to ask, 'Are you a butt sorcerer?' That, *that*, my lady, is why I must kill."

"Wouldn't that story make more sense if instead of killing Mortimer, you asked if he was—I can't believe I'm even entertaining this—a butt sorcerer?" asked Pantsa incredulously.

Dog Shit looked at her without a single glint of understanding in his eyes. The lords and ladies sat in uncomfortable silence.

"Yes, well, now that Dog Shit has given his…thoughtful piece," Beerion began.

"You are not here to speak!" Dog Shit yelled as he pulled the chain taught, forcing Beerion to his knees.

"Why have you brought the Imp?" asked Whoremund while digging his single tooth into a not fully dead wild boar.

"He is our prisoner," said Dog Shit, face full of regret as he looked at the wild boar's butthole with envy.

"Speaking of prisoners…where is my brother?" asked Malarya.

"We have not decided what to do with him yet," replied Dog Shit sternly.

"If you lay a finger on my brother, I will cut your throat," Malarya said, not batting an eye.

"Easy, Malarya," calmed Beerion. "It is understandable that the Funsullied want your brother to receive some sort of punishment for killing their queen."

"Beerion, I will cut *your* throat using Dog Shit's throat!" Malarya threatened.

"Silence!" cried Dog Shit. "This city is ours. We will decide what to do with our prisoners."

"It's not for you to decide," Beerion coughed out, getting back up on his feet.

"I am the commander of the Funsullied. You are my prisoner. We will decide Jon Dough's punishment. If there is a problem with that, you can kiss my butt—" Dog Shit cut himself off, choking back tears as he reminded himself of his buttless predicament.

"You buttless bastards don't get to decide shit!" said Whoremund between bites of his second wild boar. "You've never taken a shit! Hahaha," he slurped. "And in any case, who is to decide then? Me? No, no. Not me. Certainly not, that wouldn't make any sense. I am not king!"

"We have no king! Nor queen…anymore," said Pantsa.

"You people are the most powerful lords and ladies in Westopolis," said Beerion. "Pick one."

Beerion's words resounded in the air for a moment. It seemed that among the burning remains of King's Landing Strip, a seedling of rebirth could emerge from the middle of these sitting lords and ladies.

"I mean, I'll do it," said Whoremund, standing up nonchalantly, wiping hog grease off of his face and burping. "If no one else wants to, I'll be king."

"My king, I will serve you until death." Ser Boats McSeaman removed his sword from his sheath and knelt, plunging it into the dirt. He bowed his head. Ser Boats, being extremely nonconfrontational, could not handle the idea of an argument breaking out between the lords and ladies, all of whom he considered his best friends. He was willing to let Whoremund's lackluster display slide and serve him until death.

"Certainly not *Whoremund*," said Beerion, rolling his eyes.

"I suppose you're wanting it to be you then, eh?" retorted Whoremund.

"Me? The Imp, who killed his mother, his father, and by association his sister and brother? The man who has had his hands in all the wars, the violence, and the tragedy our Seven Kingdoms have experienced? The man who half the world hates for supporting Dennys and the other half hates for betraying her?"

"Yes, my king!" Ser Boats groveled, now pivoting to bow toward Beerion instead.

"I cannot think of a worse choice," said Beerion, lowering his head in shame.

Suddenly Ham Tardy stood up. "My lords. My ladies. What if... well, what I mean to say is this: what if instead of choosing a king or queen, we develop an intricate system of communal labor forces that, while self-sufficient, will produce goods at a surplus that can be used to fund and feed an army, as well as various social welfare programs such as universal health care and standardized free education? What if we worked together to write a book relating the economic concepts of scaled production and public ownership of capital and then used said book to guide our political structure?"

"Ham, are you quite finished being a dumb fat guy so that we might get on with this?" said Pantsa.

"Shut up, Ham," said Ser Boats. All the lords and ladies laughed at Ham until he sat back down. Then they began laughing even harder at the sound the chair made when he sat. It was kind of like a "gerffff," or more like a "squeebie squeebie." It's a hard sound to describe, but it was hilarious.

"Who then?!" screamed Whoremund, biting his own hand because he was eating boar so fast. "Who will be king?!"

"I have had nothing but time to think these past few weeks while all of you have been journeying here," began Beerion.

"Oh, and what a journey it was! At one point I looked at a rock!" said Whoremund.

"Yes, I am sure you did. But I know one of us who has looked at quite a bit more. Bland the Broken. You have seen our past. All of ours. And all of it. You can see the present, anywhere in the world, with just the shutting of your eyes. You know what the future will hold before it happens. You know what all of us look like naked."

"Hold on, Beerion," said Pantsa, shifting uncomfortably. "You don't mean to suggest that my brother should rule the Seven Kingdoms? Nothing against you, Bland, but are you up to the task? Do not let this Imp put you into a position where you feel you cannot refuse."

"Your brother is what is best for this world, Pantsa. I know he does not want this responsibility. And it is for that very reason that he must accept."

"I will serve you, my king," said Ser Boats, unsurprisingly.

The lords and ladies were quiet for a moment. Then Whoremund stood. He looked around to see if anyone had some food they were not finished with. None. "Ah, what the hell, my king!"

"Well, I suppose a boy with the collective memory of everyone is as close to a collective leadership as we will get, huh," said Ham pathetically with a little chuckle.

"Shut. Up. Ham," said Dog Shit. "But, fine. The boy can be king."

The lords and ladies continued to stand and give their support for Bland Snark. He sat emotionless, looking to Pantsa, the last one remaining seated. She toiled with her fingers for a moment before looking up to the group.

"The North will remain independently ruled. As we have for thousands of years. And as we will for thousands more."

Bland nodded, emitting a small smile.

"Well then, Bland. You have heard the lords and ladies speak. What do you say, will you be our king?" questioned Beerion.

There was a silent energy filling the air as everyone looked to Bland. Even Dog Shit leaned in, patiently awaiting the boy's answer.

"Why do you think I've been so annoying this whole time?" Bland smirked smugly. "I accept."

"And so it is settled! Bland Snark, the Pink-Eyed Raven, will lead Westopolis into a glorious golden age the likes of which has never been seen before. He will rule justly, free from the clouds of envy and greed that have afflicted so many kings before him. Tell us, Your Grace, what will be your first acts as king?"

"Firstly, Beerion, you are to be my Best Man."

"No," Beerion chuckled nervously, "I'm afraid my days of politics are surely behind me, Your Grace."

"You have had your hand in all the decisions of the most powerful people in Westopolis for the greater half of your life. You have spent your days making many mistakes. Now you will spend the rest of your days fixing them." Bland's words were spoken with such calm authority that Beerion found himself unable to formulate a clever protest. Instead he blurted out, "Righty-o, Mr. Kingy-o," and then immediately shook his head and wondered where in the seven hells *that* came from.

"Now then, as to the matter of my brother Jon." Bland looked around the circle of chairs and was greeted by a full gambit of facial expressions. It seemed that if Jon lived, half the lords and ladies would be furious, and if he died, the other half would be furiouser. "Jon will be sent north of the Trench to live with the Mildlings."

Whoremund stood up and burped up a few chickens. "Aye! So the lad will finally become one of us after all! Three cheers for the fair King Bland. Hip Hip Hoora—"

"Hold on! No one who murders a queen I vowed to protect keeps his life. Not even a main character." Dog Shit stood indignantly, scowling at Bland and Whoremund. He readied his spear.

A bead of sweat dripped down Bland's forehead. "Now, hold on, hold on. You didn't let me finish. Um, Jon Dough will be sent north of the Trench, where he will be murdered by his own direwolf, Toast. Happy?"

"Bland, you monster!" Malarya sprung up. "You cannot do this to our brother!"

"I did not finish!" Bland stammered. "He will be killed *metaphorically* by Toast, who will in a literal sense only pester him with constant pleas for attention. There. It is decided."

"That is no punishment. He has to pet his dog? What the hell kind of punishment is that?" Dog Shit grew angry.

"If you people would let me finish, please! As I was saying, it is decided that, uh, it is *not* decided . . . Because, um, Beerion?" Bland quickly wanked in his mind to mentally escape. Now he was in a strip club in Wintersmells that he particularly fancied.

"Dough will be a Mildling until the day that he dies. It is justice as it is as good as death as far as we should be concerned. But if anything, it is not merciful enough, given his actions to save the realm from yet another tyrant," Beerion said.

"Not merciful enough?! The only mercy I will show him will be when I kill him before cutting off his butt-hole!" screamed Dog Shit.

Bickering between the lords and ladies continued until nightfall, but eventually Bland returned from his mental paradise and squared everything away. Jon was to be exiled to north of the Trench with the Mildlings. Pantsa would rule the North independently. Ser Boats McSeaman would receive reparations in the form of a new reading tutor with free lessons twice a week. That final stipulation was the result of several hours of harsh negotiations.

Everyone began packing their supplies and settling in for the night before the long journey back the next morning.

"Geez," said one of the lords, scratching his head as he was heading out, "is anyone else having second thoughts about making Bland the king? Like, does anyone else think this is an unsatisfying way to wrap up this chapter of our lives? Or does anyone feel just kind of disappointed that this is how we're ending things?"

Everyone shrugged and kept preparing to head home.

Pantsa approached Malarya and put a loving hand on her shoulder.

"Let's go get some rest, sister. It will be a long day of travel tomorrow back to Wintersmells."

"No, I will not be returning to Wintersmells. It smells of winter there," said Malarya as she studied a mysterious map.

"What?"

Malarya wrested her eyes from the map to meet her sister's concerned glance. "Listen, I have no place being a Lady of Wintersmells anymore. That's not me. I must follow my heart and answer the call I hear so constantly. I am going west to explore."

"West? But what is west of Westopolis?"

"What is west of Westopolis indeed, sister . . ." Malarya grinned and looked to the setting sun. "That is what I shall find out." *And hopefully kill some people*, she thought to herself.

⤞⤝

Dawn broke early. Malarya and her crew had already been up for hours preparing her new ship, fondly named in memory of her father, the HMS *Decapitated Sack of Bones*, for its journey west.

"Eyes up, lads! Hoist the poop deck and foil the masts!" Malarya commanded. Her knowledge of boats was nonexistent, but her confidence inspired the crew of hardened sailors into swift action.

When all was ready, King Bland christened the ship from the shore with a keg, powerfully thrown at the weakest part of the boat. It was such a powerful throw that the keg went straight through the boat, flying out the other side, leaving a giant hole.

"Now the boat has an indoor pool!" shouted Malarya optimistically. "Thanks, Bland!"

Malarya stood at the helm and shouted down to her crew.

"Anchors aweigh! Today we sail for adventure!" The crew cheered. "Today we sail for glory!" The crew cheered louder and began waving their shirts over their heads. "Today we may die in the name of pointless exploration!" They put their shirts back on nervously.

The ship began to move out of the harbor, into the thick fog that constantly loomed over the shallows to the west. Slowly, it dipped into the fog and disappeared.

"What in the seven hells will you have for me out here, you bastard of a sea?" Malarya said to herself.

Half a second later, the ship shuddered and halted, and Malarya's first mate called out, "We have run aground, my lady."

"We have—what?" Malarya was in disbelief. Suddenly all the fog cleared from their view ahead. In front of them lay a massive, beautiful continent. Waterfalls fell from high cliffs into pools of crystal blue water. Every type of animal imaginable, and some that even the most creative author could not be bothered to describe, grazed lush plains for as far as the eye could see. Inland a few hundred yards there were multitudes of fruit-bearing trees just coming into bloom. Plentiful reserves of gold and silver could be seen dotting the cliffside.

"Are you fucking kidding me? How could nobody have ever known this existed?" Malarya scrambled to her maps. All of them had things like "Eh, there's nothing here, buddy boy" or "Who cares—it's probably just fog forever" written where the continent was.

"Send word to my brother immediately."

"That's okay. I can hear you from here!" Bland said from shore.

~❧~

In the following weeks, the realm enjoyed an uncharacteristic period of peace and prosperity. Bland managed to lower taxes while simultaneously creating thousands of new jobs for peasants—jobs such as poop shoveler, shovel maker, poop producer, and tax attorney.

On the surface, the realm had never seen such positive progress. Yet, in the privacy of the newly reconstructed and newly handicap-accessible Red Queef, King Bland issued secretive, sinister commands.

"Because I am king and what I say is law! And as the Pink-Eyed Raven, what I say is always correct. So if you would rather obey me because it is the law or because I am right, you may decide for yourself. But one thing is certain, you *will* obey me!" Bland sat on the corner of his bed, yelling at a wind-up toy that had stopped working. Giving up, he threw the toy against the wall, shattering it into a still fully intact toy with a small dent on it. Beerion, hearing the commotion, entered swiftly.

"Your Grace, is everything alright?"

"Nevermind all that, Dwarf-Man McShortyButt!" Since becoming king, Bland had become very fond of hurling insults at all those around him. Though most were not as clever as the dagger he had just unleashed on Beerion, they all had to do with people having short butts for the most part. "How is work proceeding on Executive Order 66?" Bland rubbed his hands together maniacally and began to grin.

"Well…it proceeds. But, Your Grace—"

"I'm sorry, Beerion. Do my ears mistake me, or were you just about to question my authority? Do you know what happened to the last person who questioned my authority?"

Beerion looked with horror at the discarded wind-up toy, slightly dented, on the floor.

Just then, the commander of the Kingsguard burst into the room. "Your Grace, we got another one." He dropped a bloody wheelchair on the ground in front of him.

"Excellent. Bring it down to the melting room."

"The, um, the furnace room?"

"The MELTING room!"

"Well, it's just nobody has ever called it that before. Generally it's not used for melting, in fact. Only once you ordered us to go out into the country and murder every teenage boy in a wheelchair we could find, and then melt their chairs down into a great throne, did we melt anything down there, in all honesty." The commander had tried Bland's patience.

"Would you like to be melted along with the chair?"

"No, Your Grace. Right away." The commander scurried downstairs to the melting room.

"What is it that you have to say, Beerion?" Bland asked, reading Beerion's concerned face.

"Your Grace...Surely you see the parallels between what you are doing and what the horrid kings and queens before you did. You have gone mad with power. These boys in their wheelchairs...they pose no threat to you."

"Oh, and I suppose I posed no threat to Cervix? To Dennys? I am king of Westopolis! A broken child from the North, leading the realm. Quite successfully, I might add."

"Why are you melting down the chairs into a new throne, though? Swords of the conquered was one thing, but defenseless boys' wheelchairs? What sort of message does that send?" Beerion tried to connect with Bland's empathetic nature.

"Do you think you are going to connect to some sort of empathetic nature inside me?" Bland snickered. "It sends the message that I am king, and the only thing that will ever stop me from being king is NOTHING. I will live to be thousands of years old as the Pink-Eyed Raven. And while I live I will never cede my rule. Who knows, I may live...*forever*!" Lightning and thunder started cracking and booming outside. "I will never die! And the Seven Kingdoms will tremble at the sound of my name: Bland the Bringer of Death! Mwahahaha! Mwahahaha!"

Gods, fucking shit, thought Beerion, severely in need of a drink. *I guess this is it. This was a horrible mistake. Bland? As king? That doesn't even make sense. What was I thinking? What a truly disappointing, nonsensical, unsatisfactory way for all of this to end.*

LeBronn

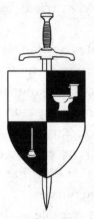

Did somebody say, 'Damn, that guy is badass'?!"
LeBronn burst through the door of King
Bland's newly constructed throne room, wield-
ing a javelin in one hand and a matte-black machete in
the other.

"Yes, my lord. King Bland has ordered me to repeat
that to him for several hours now," spoke a lowly peasant
boy. The boy was fanning Bland with a palm branch and
complimenting him while he sat in his new wheelchair
throne, admiring his crown.

"I've been expecting you, LeBronn. Oh, Beerion, it
seems your precious sellsword friend has finally come to
dethrone me. I can't imagine this is any of *your* doing, is
it?" Bland smirked.

"LeBronn, what are you doing?!" stammered Beerion. He suddenly stopped polishing King Bland's feet. "Your Grace, I assure you I had no idea he was coming."

"Why, then, did I discover this raven you sent to LeBronn's homestead telling him to return to the Strip immediately and kill the 'tyrant king who has gone mad with power'?"

"Well, I—surely no such raven existed..."

"Save me your ignorant attempts to save yourself. Once I deal with this pathetic 'threat,' I will cut your throat myself. Bring it on, LeBronn. You are no match for my Pink-Eyed Raven laser eyes!"

LeBronn hurled his javelin straight through Bland's heart. "Ah, that's right...I don't have laser eyes. But I did see that coming." Bland keeled over dead.

"LeBronn, what were you thinking? That was far too close for comfort. I told you to come in the middle of night and do the deed while he was asleep!" Beerion wiped the sweat from his forehead.

"Whatever, sweet cheeks. I'm the author's favorite character. I can do whatever I want." *Hey there, readers, George here. LeBronn didn't actually say this, but it would be so cool if he did, right? God, I fucking love that guy.*

LeBronn tossed Bland into a heap on the floor and sat on the throne. "This I could get used to."

"Well, of course *you* will not become king!" Beerion was shocked. "I promised you a castle filled with gold and whores if you could slay Bland."

"No one has a grander castle, more gold, or more beautiful whores than the king, old friend." LeBronn placed the crown on his head.

"But this is entirely unorthodox! The people will never accept you as their king. It just could never work. Would you *please* stop fanning, boy!"

"No, no. Please continue. It feels delightful."

Beerion stared at LeBronn with disgust for a moment and then stormed out of the room. LeBronn rolled his eyes as Beerion slammed the door.

"Very well. Fan Boy, you will be appointed my Best Man. And for my first act as king, I order you to round up all the women to the west and bring them to this room. And don't get comfortable because my second act is going to be to order you to round up all the women to the east."

※

"That doesn't sound good at all," Ham said worriedly, putting down his book.

"Exactly," cried Beerion. "That is what I am trying to tell you. LeBronn cannot be king. I just needed him to help remove Bland so that we could install a proper, just ruler for the realm! Now hurry. I have no doubt LeBronn will send men looking for us soon. There must be something in all of these books that can help us! There must be a prophecy or some other more clever plot device of some sort that will name the rightful king. Who should we turn to for leadership?!" Beerion anxiously peeked under the door of the library, watching for torchlight coming down the hallway.

"Didn't you say Bland was the true, proper, just leader for the realm at that meeting a few weeks ago?" Ham asked.

"Ham! I was drunk when I said that!"

"But you're drunk now!"

"And thank the Gods for that. But we have no time for this! Surely, somewhere... *one* of these books." Beerion flipped through all the books on Ham's desk. "No, no, Ham! All of these are cookbooks."

"Actually most of them are just pictures of food, but—"

"Ham this is important. Think."

"Well, I suppose..." Ham drifted off.

"What?! What is it?"

"There is the fan theory message board scroll. But, no. We mustn't."

"Excellent. We must. What is that?" Beerion grabbed Ham by the shin and pleaded for a response.

"There is a scroll, you see. A scroll that ranks the names of everyone born of noble blood in Westopolis by their likelihood of becoming king. A scroll that magically updates at about 9 p.m. every Sunday. It has always been dismissed as nothing more than hogwash, but I suppose..."

"Ham, this is perfect. Who is at the top of the list?!"

"Well, it's Jon of course. It has always been Jon Dough."

"Ham, get me a raven. No, to send a message, not to eat. Gods, how long has that been in your pocket, man?"

Jon

Where is he?!" shouted Jon, hurtling up the stairs toward the Chair Room. Beerion was sitting on his shoulder, hanging onto a strand of Jon's hair for dear life.

"In the Chair Room. I already told you. That is why we are on our way there now."

"Good. And where is the Chair Room?!" Jon screamed as he kicked down the door to the Chair Room.

"Looks like you found it, sweet cheeks. Does that catchphrase still work?" LeBronn asked his Best Man.

"Yes, Your Grace. Even better the second time," the boy said, continuing to fan LeBronn.

"You killed my brother, you monster. And now you dare to sit on his throne while it is still wet from his accidents. Prepare to die." Jon drew his sword, and Beerion hopped off his shoulders.

"Is that what this is? I figured it was some sort of king thing to sit on a waterbed-chair hybrid. Either way, your brother went mad with power the day he got it. If you ask me, I'm twice the king he ever could have been. Even without that whole omnipotence schtick he had going for him." LeBronn causally stood up and prepared his own sword. Jon smiled and put his sword to the ground. "Giving up that easy, Jon?"

Jon put his fingers to his lips and let out an ear-piercing whistle. Toast exploded through the open door and lunged at LeBronn. Before LeBronn could get in a swing at the wolf, Toast ripped his neck off. LeBronn, the best character in the book, was tragically dead. "Who's a good boy? Who's a Toasty, Toasty boy?" Jon pet Toast's stomach.

Ham came waddling up the stairs into the throne room. "Jon! It is so good to see you."

"Hello, Ham." Jon grew somber looking at the decaying heap of Bland's body on the ground.

"Sorry, Jon. I've been meaning to move that. It's just every time I make it to the top of these stairs, I am so exhausted—anyway. According to this scroll that Beerion and I uncovered...you are to be king! King of Westopolis, the Sandals, and the Thirsty Men, all of that!"

Just then, Dog Shit rushed into the room and plunged his spear clean through Jon Dough's heart.

"Dog Shit, what have you done?!" cried Ham.

"Jon Dough had to pay for his crimes against Dennys Grandslam. I could not stand by and watch him get away

277

with the murder of two sworn leaders!" Dog Shit bowed honorably.

"But LeBronn was by no means a sworn leader!" Beerion pleaded.

"Maybe so. But I, Dog Shit, commander of the Funsullied, haver of no butt, will be. I claim my right to the throne."

"Well, now...actually that may not be so." Ham unfurled the scroll. "In the case of Jon's death, the king is—ha!"

"Who?! Who is this alleged king?!" Dog Shit swore furiously.

"Well, in fact it is—"

Toast

Awww. *Now* look at him!" Ham clapped giddily, smiling from ear to ear.

"All we have done is look at him for the past forty-five minutes! Thirty minutes of which he was licking himself, and now he's just walking in stupid circles!" Dog Shit spat at Ham.

"Because he's trying to find a good spot to lay down, Dog Shit—it's cuuute." Ham batted his eyelashes playfully, fawning over Toast. "Also, what was that you just said? 'Minutes'? What in the seven hells is that? We measure time in lengths of the late King Robot Boaratheon's feet. What are you on about?"

"I don't know, I was just trying something out..."

"Well, it'll never stick."

Stick! The stick Toast was happily gnawing on snapped. He lazily rolled over and settled in to lick himself once again.

"A dog cannot be the king. This, as well as several times before this, is where I draw the line."

Ham cocked a confident smirk. "Well, I'm sorry Dog Shit, but it's right here in the scroll, and seeing as you can't do anything to change that, I suggest you start showing a little more respect toward Toasty here."

Eddddd

eally?" shouted Beerion. "A dog? You killed a dog?" Ham was weeping in the corner.

"Now am I king?" asked Dog Shit, holding Toast's bloody corpse.

"Oh boy," said Ham, consulting the scroll. "Technically Eddddd is next in line as interim king."

Dog Shit threw the animal corpse on the ground in frustration.

"Alright!" shouted Eddddd, creeping in from the edge of the room where he'd been watching. "You mean Jon really had me in there as his official first best *human* friend?"

"This isn't a ranking of friends," said Ham. "It's a lineage of people most likely to end up as king. According to the people, you were less fit to rule than a dog."

Eddddd laughed. "Whatever, Ham, or perhaps I should say...Whatever, *Not-Jon's-best-human-friend*."

"You take that back!" said Ham.

"King's don't do take-backs, and I'm king!" said Eddddd, placing the crown on his head.

"Lads," said Whoremund, chewing on Toast's corpse from the side of the room. "Why are we fighting about this? The answer is obvious. *I* was Jon's best human friend!"

"I'm the king, and what I say goes," retorted Eddddd. "I officially decree that I was Jon Dough's best human friend! And anyone who says otherwise will be hanged. Understood?"

Ham and Whoremund nodded in silence.

Oh, I could get used to this, thought Eddddd, looking over his kingdom as Dog Shit promptly cut his head off.

Whoremund

I 'll be taking this," said Dog Shit, placing the crown on his head.

"This cannot keep happening! The saga needs to *end*!" shouted Ham.

"Be that as it may, surely I am the king now. Who else could possibly challenge my leadership potential?"

"Agh, about *that*," squeaked Ham, pointing at Whoremund and mouthing the words "next in line."

"A Mildling? As king?" asked Dog Shit.

"You got a problem with that?" said Whoremund, yanking the crown away from Dog Shit and putting it on his own head. *Wait, he's right. Who on Wearth* (which, by the way, is what Earth is called in this universe—sorry, I forgot to write that in earlier, damn) *had a progressive-enough mind to think that I would be king, given how poorly Mild-lings have been treated?* thought Whoremund.

"I'm just reading what's here on the scroll, folks. Also, Whoremund, he's definitely going to try to kill you right now."

Dog Shit unsheathed his sword and began making his way toward Whoremund. Whoremund quickly responded to what Ham had said. *It's on the scroll,* he thought. *It's canon. I, a Mildling, am king.* Whoremund began to launch into an impassioned speech about how this was a historic day for Mildling rights, one sentence into which his throat was cut by Dog Shit.

Ham

"Now?" asked Dog Shit.

Ham looked down at the scroll and saw his own name. He tucked it under his arm and took off sprinting as fast as he could waddle.

"Ham?!" shouted Dog Shit, chasing after him. "Get back here, book boy!"

Ham bounded across the Strip to the only place he felt safe—the library. Once inside, he locked the metal doors behind him just in time to stop Dog Shit.

Phew, thought Ham. *That was a close one. Now, I'll just live inside this library forever so Dog Shit can't kill me. It won't be so bad. I'll read books all day. I'll get food ... somehow.*

Dog Shit cut through the metal doors with his knife with ease. He cut out a large hole for himself and walked in.

"Book boy! Are you king?"

"Uhhhhh," panicked Ham, looking around. "No!" he shouted, spotting Ser Boats McSeaman in the children's section of the library. "Ser Boats is! It's Ser Boats and he's my friend and that's why I didn't want to tell you!"

Boats

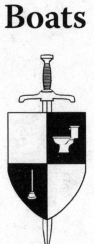

Hey, what's going on over there?" said Ser Boats McSeaman, upset by the commotion at the front of the library. "I'm trying to learn to read over here, and I'm almost done with the *Z* words!"

"You're the king now!" shouted Ham.

"Huh?" said Boats, getting speared in the heart by Dog Shit. With his last breath, Boats looked at his "King Arthur Learn-to-Read and Stickers" book and croaked out, "Zee...zee...zebra." But he pronounced it oh so wrong.

Dog Shit

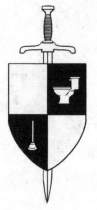

It had been one week since all the killing. Dog Shit stood at his throne, wearing his new crown, commanding throngs of Funsullied.

"We will cut the butts off every infidel!"

The audience went wild with cheers as Ham hid in the corner. Suddenly, Dog Shit stopped speaking because the tip of a long knife was protruding from his chest. It had been stuck into him by Malarya Snark.

"Attack!" she shouted. Out came every single lord and lady in all of Westopolis, called upon by Ham via emergency raven messages to retake the crown.

What followed was the bloodiest battle in the history of the Strip. It had now been zero weeks since the most recent killing. Hundreds of thousands died, and the bloodshed attracted Dragun back to the Strip. It was his first time returning since Dennys's death, and the memory of her murder was fresh in his mind. He unleashed a devastating rain of fire, incinerating nearly all the remaining survivors and reducing the city to a pile of rubble once more.

Pantsa

Pantsa, Malarya, Ham, and Beerion sat on the ashy ground. They were the only survivors of the battle and the ensuing dragon attack. Around them was rubble and not much else. There was nothing left to fight over and no one left to fight over it. The four decided that for the sake of preserving a shred of order and decency, they would name Pantsa queen. She stood up, took a deep breath of smoky, ash-ridden air, and before she could deliver a speech died of pulmonary complications due to mesothelioma.

Screw It: Malarya, Ham, and Beerion

lright then. You wanna do it? The whole queen thing?" Beerion asked Malarya.

"Nope."

Ham suddenly perked up and spoke with the air of a whimsical whistle. "Well, alright then, who says anyone needs to rule us? Why, I'm sure we could get by on our own! We could go on all sorts of cheery, wacky adventures together! We could see the world!"

"Adventure!" chirped Malarya.

"And exotic liquor and women!" grinned Beerion.

"Just the three of us sticking up for each other, exploring this great fantasy world we call home! The way it's always been!" Ham smiled from ear to ear. Strings began to swell, and the sky turned golden while the sun slowly dipped beneath the horizon.

"One for all!"

"And all for one!"

Suddenly the sky turned dark. The violins abruptly stopped, followed awkwardly by the cellos, who were not paying attention to the conductor. In the distance, a dark figure drew his sword. Before Malarya could make a move to defend the three, the sword came flying at their necks. It spun through each one like a sword cutting through butter, and then flesh, and then bone. Ham's coat had some butter on it. They collapsed to the ground without any final words.

Epilogue

The figure approached the three fresh corpses he'd made. As he walked, he surveyed the fractured remnants of the city.

The horizon was no longer visible for all the smoke. Hundreds of thousands of bodies—the entire population of the Strip—lay strewn about and smoldering. Their corpses told of the sad final moments of a broken city: mothers reaching for children who reached for a salvation that wasn't there.

He walked down the steps to the red-light district. Doorways sheltered darkened figures, much of their bodies reduced to ash, their palms stretched into the brothels and holding coins that had melted and fused onto their skin, the bodies halted in their attempts to find a last bit of happiness as their worlds burned around them. He stepped over the many horses that lay before the buildings, still hitched to their posts, their faces frozen in grotesque screams.

He stopped before a small structure and seemed to consider something for a moment before looking up at it, his hesitation betraying some familiarity with the building. He stepped into the structure's one room and saw building blocks and painted dolls littering the floor. There were many small mounds on the floor, and in the corner he saw one mound that was larger than the rest. He approached this large mound, and as he did so he saw that it was a corpse. He shifted it a bit and realized that it was actually two corpses: an adult shielding a child. He looked at the child and saw that it was holding a small wooden figure of a knight on a horse. The details of the figure had been spared, protected from the dragon's fires by the soft flesh of the child's arm. It was a very fine figure, with exquisite attention given to the details in the armor of both rider and horse. It looked as though at any moment it might breathe and charge into some legendary battle. It would have been the greatest possession of any schoolchild. He picked the figure out of the child's grasp, and as he did so it crumbled into dust. He stood up and walked past the mounds—corpses, he now knew—and out of the school building.

He continued his walk and finally arrived at the small square where he had launched his sword. Three figures lay crumpled on the ground, a mess of cloth and outstretched limbs, a small but growing pool of blood beneath them. He cleaned off his sword, resheathed it, and then knelt to consider the bodies for a moment. They were so young. Too young to have been playing this game.

At Ham's feet sat the crown. The figure picked it up and manipulated it in his hands. *So much death, for this little thing*...he thought. He stared at the crown for a few minutes more and then placed it on his head, cleared his throat, and spoke:

"Well if that ain't just a game of thrones!" laughed Trashbag—Eldest Son of Winston Garbagio, First to Collect Trash Inside Himself like a Bag, First to Consider Changing His Name to Something More Kingly Now That He Had Appearances to Uphold, First to Change His Name to "Tra$hbag," First to Be Currently Shimmying Across the Corpses of Malarya and Ham and Beerion and Fist Pumping the Crown in the Air, First to Skip Across a Field Shouting "I'm da King, I'm da Queen!" and then Tripping and Falling Really Hard, First to Stay Down for a Scary Amount of Time, First to Slowly Get Up and Say "...*and* da Prince!" and Then Absolutely Eat Shit Again, First to Roll Over and Groan "and...and... da...Princess" Through the Sudden Bear Mauling He Was Receiving, First to Seem Almost Certainly Dead and Then Cough Up Too Much Blood Two Hours Later but It Gets All Up His Nose and He Starts Choking Again, First to Crawl Home to His Dog and Say "Talk About a Ruff Day," First to Collapse in Bed Thinking to Himself "Finally, Time to Relax" and Smile, Last to Realize He Left the Crown in the Field Fifty Miles Back, and the One True King of the Seven Municipalities.

Appendix

House
Boaratheon

House
Snark

House
Bangsister

House
Thighspell

House
Playboy

House
Grandslam

House
Ofpain

House
Martin

About the *Harvard Lampoon*

The *Harvard Lampoon* was founded in 1876 and is among the oldest continually published humor magazines in history. It has been an incubator for some of the brightest and most respected names in comedy—including Conan O'Brien, Colin Jost, Lawrence O'Donnell, B. J. Novak, Patricia Marx, Susan Borowitz, Alan Yang, Amy Ozols, Andy Borowitz, Ian Frazier, dozens of SNL writers, writers and producers of *Atlanta*, *Veep*, *The Office*, *Parks and Recreation*, *30 Rock*, and almost every *Simpsons* writer ever. Earlier alumni include John Updike, George Plimpton, William Gaddis, George Santayana, William Randolph Hearst, and Robert Sherwood. The *Lampoon*'s 1969 Tolkien parody *Bored of the Rings* is the bona fide classic of the form, and its success spurred the founding of the *National Lampoon*. More recently, *Twilight* parody *Nightlight* and *Hunger Games* parody *The Hunger Pains* both became *New York Times* best sellers. Each parody is written by a new group of Harvard students who have joined the *Lampoon*.

Credits for *Lame of Thrones*:
Head writers: Juan Arenas, Mike Miller, and Jack Stovitz
Writers: Jakob Gilbert, Zach Goddard, Lia Kiam, Brian Mott, Michael Perusse, Scott Roberts, Posy Stoller, and James Wolfe
Cover art, map, and sigils: Isabel Gibney
In-book drawings: Nicole Araya
Additional material: Freddie Shanel and Grace Shi